No Prayer,
No Power

AMBER R. MORSON

No Prayer, No Power: Prayers to start every day of the year.

© 2017 by Amber R. Morson

www.advisedbyamber.com

Printed in the United States of America

ISBN-13: 978-0999270905
ISBN-10: 0999270907

Library of Congress Cataloging-in-Publication Data
LCCN: 2017914990

Cover design by Increase Branding & Design | www.increase.design
Headshot by AGM Productions | Instagram: @agm.productions

To the reader,
prayer is only powerful if you use it.

Special Thanks

It is a great feeling to see God's vision for my life unfolding through completion of this prayer book. I pray that out of my obedience comes strength, miracles, and blessings for all who read. I would like to thank God for using me as a vessel for his glory. For seeing me as worthy enough to take on such a great and delicate responsibility. I do not take this calling or influence lightly.

I am forever grateful for my dream team!

My parents, Pastor Doran Morson and Elder Sylvia Morson, who are just indescribable. I know that God favored me because he gave me you. I appreciate all the sacrifices you have made.

My astute editor and uncle, Pastor D.L. Harville, who graced my prayers with his power and pen. I pray God continues to bless you for being a blessing to me. My sister, Dalisa, your help in the final editing stage made all the difference.

My late Bishop White and Overseer White, who instilled in me the power of prayer and inspired my book title "No Prayer, No Power."

My village and accountability partners: my immediate family - Dj, Dalisa, Bailee, all those who played a part in encouraging me through the writing process, Higher Praise Ministries, Inc. (Detroit, MI), family, friends, sorors, and a host of others - I sincerely appreciate you!

To the naysayers, whose purpose was to push me closer to mine, thank you!

Foreword

Doran Morson, Sr.
Higher Praise Ministries, Inc. | Senior Pastor

Prayer is one of the most powerful and fundamental aspects of the Christian life. We cannot expect growth in grace without time in prayer. This book *No Prayer, No Power* gives readers an important and wonderful insight to how we communicate with God through prayer. After reading this book, you will form a closer bond and gain direct entrance to God's answer to your prayers. You will find prayers for strength, healing, direction, and many of life's daily needs.

What I found to be an essential quality of prayer is persistence. Jesus taught in Luke 18:1 that men ought to always pray and not get tired. This lesson should motivate us to pray and to pray persistently. It is important to separate a special time to be alone with God daily where we can turn our burdens, needs and cares over to Him. It is not enough for us to talk about God, we must begin to speak to God.

Prayer is one of the most fundamental and one of the most forgotten aspects of the Christian life. It is time for us to make a dedication to daily spiritual exercises that build our spiritual life with Christ, such as prayer. This 365-day prayer book is the beginning point to establishing a fruitful prayer life and a stronger relationship with God.

Matthew 7:7-8 declares, "Ask, and it shall be given to you; seek, and you shall find; knock, and it shall be opened to you. For everyone who asks receives, and he who seeks finds, and to him who knocks it shall be opened."

No Prayer, No Power is a book that asks, seeks, and knocks on the closed doors of life. *No Prayer, No Power* is a book that teaches you how to ask God for help and direction. It will show you how to seek God daily. You will soon experience the closed doors in your life open because you have trusted God through prayer.

When you read this book, it takes you to a place of prayer that gets God's attention. This book will be beneficial for those who seek a better prayer life. Let this book be a tool for how to communicate with God when you do not know how or what to say to Him.

This book was inspired by the Spirit of God through the writer who at an early age learned that prayer works and that God does answer prayers. Let this book be the bridge to the next level of your prayer life.

Introduction

There was a time when I knew I needed to talk to God. I tried to speak, but I just did not know what to say. My mind was overwhelmed, I was heartbroken, and essentially stuck. Shame, guilt, and disappointment replayed in my mind, and I could not shake it. At this point, everything I thought I knew about God and his word was tested.

I started seeking advice from family, friends, and anyone who would listen. I was asking for help from everyone besides the one who could provide the answer. As a result, came more confusion and stress. All along I knew that my only way out of this dark space was through my faith in God.

So, I began to pray my way out. For the first couple of weeks, all I did was cry apologetically to God. Then I began to cry with thanksgiving because I expected a shift in my circumstances. Immediately, I felt stronger, wiser, grateful, and free. I had tapped into the power of the Holy Spirit through prayer. Prayer will free you from bondage. It will strengthen, guide and protect you. It is our spiritual life line. Prayer is powerful because it is our direct access to communicate with God and receive his power.

God was with me through it all – he heard it all, he saw it, and he truly cared. Once I realized that I was carrying the weight of my sins and issues, I released them to God. It is what he died for, to bear our sins, so we do not have to. What are you carrying that God's asking you to release? How much more are you going to take, when God just wants you to trust?

This prayer book was conceived from a place of pain, but I decree and declare that it is now birthed to bless! As you pray these prayers, do so out loud with boldness and expectation. Do so with an open mind, heart, and, spirit ready to receive all God has for you. Get ready to experience God's presence, his peace, and power. Get ready to renew your strength and activate your faith.

I pray that as you pray, you experience joy like no other. I pray that you become stronger in your faith so no matter what life brings, you live by God's word. I pray that you come to know who you were created to be in Christ Jesus. That in knowing you find the confidence to live life in abundance. I pray that you understand the power of prayer and the simplicity of it.

If a prayer does not resonate with what you are going through, intercede on behalf of someone else. Share the goodness of Jesus Christ in the lives of those who we know need it.

Rest assured knowing that God will get the glory. Understand that his promises are true to them that believe in his son Jesus – if you do not believe you will not receive.

Be Blessed!
Amber R. Morson

Prayer > Anything
Pray without ceasing.
1 Thessalonians 5:17 (KJV)

God, I come to you asking you to fill me with a desire to pray every day. I know that prayer is the catalyst for a closer relationship with you. It is prayer and my faith in you that will change the direction of my life for the better. I understand that the enemy does not want me to pray because it is my greatest defense against him.

Give me the strength to pray before I do anything. Help me to seek you first in all things so that my life will glorify you. Forgive me for seeking the opinions and advice of others before asking yours.

I decree and declare that this year prayer will be second nature to me. I decree and declare that I will never stop praying and being thankful. Help me to be confident in knowing that you hear and answer my prayers. God, I trust that the answers to my prayers are done in the way that you see fit even if I do not agree. Help me to pray boldly. Take the fear and shyness away from me.

When the devil tries to shut my mouth, give me the words to speak. Help me to remember the prayers you have answered so that doubt will have no place in my prayer life. Help me to pray about all things. I pray that this *No Prayer, No Power* book be the jump start to a new faithful and fruitful prayer life.

In Jesus' name, I pray. Amen.

Appreciate Me

Therefore, my dear brothers and sisters, stand firm. Let nothing move you. Always give yourselves fully to the work of the Lord, because you know that your labor in the Lord is not in vain.
1 Corinthians 15:58 (NIV)

God, I know you see me, but sometimes I feel like no one does. I do not do things to get recognized or even praised. I am a decent person, and I have a good heart. Now and then I want to feel like I am appreciated. Help me to see that my time and effort are useful when the things that I do are pleasing to you. If I never hear thank you again for any of the things I do, strengthen me to be pleased with your appreciation of me. God, you placed value on my life, and I know that you love me.

Forgive me for the times I have overlooked people. Forgive me for when I have neglected you and failed to thank you for things you have done for my family and me. Help me to stand firm in who I am. Protect my passion and my heart so that my enthusiasm never dies because of those who do not appreciate me.

Help me to appreciate others in the same manner that I want to be appreciated. Send people into my life who will understand me and see the value that I have. Thank you for removing those who had no intentions on valuing me and were intentional about bringing me down. Help me to appreciate myself more than I do.

In Jesus' name, I pray. Amen.

Healing in the Hurt

The Lord is close to the brokenhearted; he rescues those whose spirits are crushed.
Psalms 34:18 (NLT)

I need to feel you near me pull me close and wrap me in your arms. My heart is heavy, and I come to you asking you to heal the hurt. I know that you are a God who cares for me as you said in 1 Peter 5:7. Help me to remember that all things are working together for my good. God, you created me, and you know what and who I need. Send people into my life who will love me the way that you created me to be loved. I have faith that you will not withhold any good thing from me. I thank you in advance for my blessing.

Give me the strength and courage to step back while you fix the people who have hurt me. God, I am not perfect, so I ask that you correct me too. Make me easy to love and build my trust so that I can love easily in return. Forgive me for my lack of faith as I have willingly accepted things that were never in your promise to me. You promised me kind, patient, and sacrificial love and I claim it right now in Jesus name.

I claim freedom from any heartbreak right now. I rebuke the spirit of sadness, depression, loneliness, guilt, and resentment. Fill my heart with your love, joy, comfort, and peace. I decree and declare that I am wiser, smarter, and prepared for what is to come.

In Jesus' name, I pray. Amen.

Bye Bye Baggage

So, if the Son sets you free, you will be free indeed.
John 8:36 (NIV)

God, I no longer want to be the owner of my baggage, and I am asking you to take over! My baggage is sin and all the things in my life that are a hindrance to my relationship with you. Thank you for sending your son Jesus to free me from sin. I have been a slave to sin for way too long, and today I will be free.

I remember that you have already freed me so help me to live in that freedom. I want my thoughts, mindset, actions, and words to reflect the freedom you have already given me. My past is irrelevant for in Christ I am a new creature.

If I fall into sin again help me to remember your grace and that it is sufficient. Allow me to repent and not stay in a sinful space out of convenience or habit. Reveal to me the areas of my life where I am drawn away from you because that is what causes me to sin.

I do not want the things I enjoy in life to become sinful and overshadow my time spent with you. Bring structure to my life so that I can better balance the pursuit of my dreams, job, family, school, or hobbies in a way that is pleasing to you.

In Jesus' name, I pray. Amen.

Hope Wins

*"For I know the plans I have for you," declares the Lord,
"plans to prosper you and not to harm you, plans to give
you hope and a future."*
Jeremiah 29:11 (NIV)

Lord God, having hope for the future given the current state
of the world is complicated. It seems like every day
something horrible is happening and it is frustrating and
causes my faith to weaken.

I am honest because you said in John 8:32 that the truth will
set me free. I know you hear my prayers and that when I ask
for something you will do it. God, free me today from the
spirit of hopelessness!

Help me to refocus my attention on your goodness and your
promises to me. Help me to stay hopeful when my plans do
not go accordingly knowing that you already have the perfect
route for my life.

During the times when I feel like a failure and find myself
stuck in a poverty-stricken mindset remind me that your
word says I am prosperous and that no weapon shall prosper
against me.

My future is created by the creator of the world, and I shall
live in the hope that brings.

In Jesus' name, I pray. Amen.

Perfectly Imperfect

Be perfect, therefore, as your heavenly Father is perfect.
Matthew 5:48 (NIV)

I struggle with wanting things to be perfect failing to realize that I am already perfect to you. At times, I desire to have the ideal picture, hair, clothes, car, ideas, assignment, spouse, home, and career. I even contemplate over making the perfect decision about my next moves and goals due to the fear of not meeting society's standards.

This perception of perfection has done nothing but made me compare myself to others and has rid me of my time.

Forgive me for striving for perfection and not owning my perfect identity as a kid of the kingdom. Align my thoughts with yours so I will not lose my identity by taking on the thoughts of others.

Continue to make my vessel a place where your spirit loves to stay. When people pity me for my sins or justify them with the excuse that no one is perfect, allow me to remember that you are. Place a desire in me to be better for you. Your spirit lives in me, and it is perfect so I know I can strive to be too.

In Jesus' name, I pray. Amen.

Courage Counts

Have I not commanded you? Be strong and courageous. Do not be afraid; do not be discouraged, for the Lord your God will be with you wherever you go.
Joshua 1:9 (NIV)

I have an opportunity ahead of me that will only be successful if I am courageous. Thank you, God, for opening this door, for awakening this doormat dream, and giving me a vision! You have ordered my steps, and today I will follow.

I will no longer wait for an opportunity to come that is already here. Now is my time! I decree and declare that I will not let this moment pass me by. Be with me as I execute your plan do not allow me to fail or mess up this time.

Today I take on strength, courage, and tunnel vision. Nothing will stop me this time. I am focused, and I hear you leading me – do not allow me to become discouraged. My courage is what counts, and it will keep me in the game.

I believe that things are only getting better from here. God, please provide all the other pieces to complete this puzzle. I will not be afraid because you are with me every step of the way.

In Jesus' name, I pray. Amen.

Please God

But without faith it is impossible to please him: for he that cometh to God must believe that he is, and that he is a rewarder of them that diligently seek him.
Hebrews 11:6 (KJV)

God, I want to start over. I repent of my sins and for doing things that do not please you. I accept you as my Lord and Savior. I believe that you raised Jesus from the dead and by faith this makes me saved according to Romans 10:9. For without faith I cannot please you and I desperately want you to be pleased with my life.

I invite you into my heart and ask that you give me your Spirit. Send people into my life that are diligently seeking you so that I can have positive influences around me. I want to experience more one-on-one encounters with you through prayer. In 1 John 3:22 it says that if I keep your commandments you will be pleased and will give me whatever I ask. Teach me your commandments, so I can be sure to do as you say.

Free up my time, responsibilities, and desires from things that are not pleasing to you. Fill my time up with everything that pleases you. I pray for friendships that are fun, yet pleasing to you.

In Jesus' name, I pray. Amen.

Prized Possession

But you are a chosen people, a royal priesthood, a holy nation, God's special possession, that you may declare the praises of him who called you out of darkness into his wonderful light.
1 Peter 2:9 (NIV)

God, you pulled me out of my mess for a reason. I was so far gone that I could not get myself out. I was stuck in a sunken place. However, you loved me so much that you shined your brightest light on me and darkness was immediately gone away.

Thank you for choosing me as your prized possession. I will forever tell of your goodness towards me. Allow my testimony to free those who are still stuck. Do not allow what I have been through and what I am coming out of to repeat in my family and friends lives.

God, I praise you for changing my life. I declare that my praise will defeat the enemy. Satan, you lose, and you will not do to my loved ones what you did to me. They will not be stuck in your web of sin because I have already overcome it and all glory belongs to God.

In Jesus' name, I pray. Amen.

Envy is the Enemy

And even when you ask, you don't get it because your motives are all wrong—you want only what will give you pleasure.
James 4:3 (NLT)

There is a lot of hate in the world. I do not want to contribute to it in any way, shape or form. Remove the spirit of jealousy and entitlement from me. Thank you for not answering prayers that I prayed from a place of envy and competition.

Align my motives and intentions to match the impact you want my life to have on others. Change my prayer life to be about what pleases you and not what pleases me. Give me a desire to pray for others and not just for myself.

God, you do not owe me anything for it is me who owes all to you. I submit to your will and your way, and I ask you to take over. I believe that you know what is best for me and that it will satisfy me.

Today, God, I pray your will, your way, and your timing!

In Jesus' name, I pray. Amen.

I Settled

*Since he did not spare even his own Son but gave him up
for us all, won't he also give us everything else?*
Romans 8:32 (NLT)

God all I had to do was wait on you. I do not understand why
I was in such a hurry. Control my excitement and
anxiousness so that it does not cause me to settle ever again.
Forgive me for being content with good enough when you
are able and willing to give me your absolute best.

Today, I take ownership of my habits that caused me to settle,
and I set a new standard for myself. Speak to me as I re-
evaluate my standards in a way where if I uphold them, the
best is guaranteed to manifest in my life. I decree and declare
that I will never be distracted again by things that look and
sound good. Filter my hearing and sight only recognize and
respond to your best.

You sacrificed your only child to show your unwavering love
for me. I accept your love and acknowledge your sacrifice.
Next time I am going to pray and be patient, knowing that
the best is on its way.

In Jesus' name, I pray. Amen.

Bless my Ambition

Work willingly at whatever you do, as though you were working for the Lord rather than for people.
Colossians 3:23 (NLT)

God, you placed an ambitious spirit inside me because I have a desire to be successful. Being ambitious is a ton of work, and often I am stretched in many different directions. Sometimes I think it would be better if I gave up some responsibilities to focus solely on what will make me successful.

It has become a norm to say, "I am doing me" and having a nonchalant attitude is more common than not. In Philippians 2:4, you told me to take an interest in the things of others and not just things for my benefit. Bless my ambition to be a bigger blessing to others. Help me not to view helping others as a threat or hindrance, but as a way to honor you.

Today I will take on your attitude of having love and compassion for others. Today I will perform at my very best as if all the work I do is submitted to you for approval. I will not lack ambition because you will bless me to be steadfast, unmovable, and always abounding in the work of the Lord as it says in 1 Corinthians 15:58.

In Jesus' name, I pray. Amen.

You Promised to Provide

But my God shall supply all your need according to his riches in glory by Christ Jesus.
Philippians 4:19 (KJV)

God, I do not know how you are going to get me through this. This situation is unexpected; this is nothing I could have prepared myself for. I need this opportunity. I need this blessing, money, and this breakthrough. I need you to hear and answer my prayers. You promised to provide all my needs, and I know that you will. I just ask that you calm my spirit in the process of you upholding your promise.

I am struggling to yield all control over to you, but I know it is what I must do. Today, I am making a conscious decision not to worry about it. This time I cannot take matters into my own hands because this is bigger than me.

I would have never imagined I would be in this situation, praying for this. However, I believe your word is real. I know this circumstance is nothing more than confirmation that you can do exceedingly abundantly above anything I can ask or think according to Ephesians 3:20.

Have your way, God. I trust your ability more than my own. I thank you in advance for arranging things on my behalf, for equipping me, and for handling the situation.

In Jesus' name, I pray. Amen.

I am Loved

For God so loved the world that he gave his one and only Son, that whoever believes in him shall not perish but have eternal life.
John 3:16 (NIV)

I had misplaced my focus to be on peoples' opinions of me, and this became how I saw myself. I allowed people to make me think I had to prove I was worthy of their love, respect, and time. Today, I choose to believe what you think about me, God.

You believe that I am worthy of love without me having to do or give anything to earn it. You freely love me over and over again even when I mess up. I declare that I will not die, be moved, or phased by the people I love that simply do not love me back.

I realize that I was never unloved because all the while you loved me. You loved me to the point where you allowed me to experience hurt so I could decipher between what is real and what is fake. Your sacrificial love rescued and protected me.

I will live with no regrets. I will live in the joy that being loved by someone like you brings me. I thank you for the people in my life that love me as you do.

In Jesus' name, I pray. Amen.

Weakness Comes First

But he said to me, "My grace is sufficient for you, for my power is made perfect in weakness." Therefore, I will boast all the more gladly about my weaknesses, so that Christ's power may rest on me.
2 Corinthians 12:9 (NIV)

God, sometimes I feel weak, down, and powerless. The devil has tried all he could to keep me from standing strong. He has pushed me down to my knees. Help me to see that he unknowingly pushed me in the right position to receive my strength this year.

I serve you and I know that no weapon formed against me shall prosper according to Isaiah 54:17. As hard times, trouble, sickness, and judgments come against me this year, I will not worry. I will stay on my knees and pray for the power to get up.

Weakness comes before strength so I will be proud and not ashamed of my low moments. For I am anticipating the point where your power begins to make me strong.

I look forward to the weights you will lift off me today and this year.

In Jesus' name, I pray. Amen.

Believers Are Blessed

And since we are his children, we are his heirs. In fact, together with Christ we are heirs of God's glory. But if we are to share his glory, we must also share his suffering.
Romans 8:17 (NLT)

God, I will be the first to admit that being your child has not been easy. I have experienced many ups and downs since accepting you as my Lord and Savior. However, I know that there is a blessing in being a believer!

Regardless of what I go through I am grateful to be your child. As your child, I am entitled and excited to inherit all you have promised me. You promised me power, strength, healing, peace, love, joy, wisdom, knowledge, and success. You promised to make me the head and not the tail, the lender and not the borrower according to Deuteronomy 28:13.

You promised that the impossible will be possible for me and that I will have more than I need. You promised to satisfy me with long life, to complete a good work in me, and to make all things work for my good. You promised me a spirit free from fear, and you freed me from the law of sin and death.

Today, I will live boldly in my authority as a child of God. I will accept my inheritance and live according to your word. I will not worry about the hardships today because as you overcame them, I will too.

In Jesus' name, I pray. Amen.

The Past, Passed Away

Therefore, if any man be in Christ, he is a new creature: old things are passed away; behold, all things are become new.
2 Corinthians 5:17 (KJV)

Today, I am saying my last goodbye to my past. I will not let the past keep me from living freely in who I am today. I have forgiven myself. God, you have forgiven me. For those who do not forgive me, I pray that you release the unforgiveness in their heart. I am happy and free from who I use to be.

Heal the hurt, pain, anger, and damage I have caused in my past relationships with my friends and family. Release them from their old mindsets and perceptions of me. When they try to define me presently by the things I did in my past help them to see that you renewed me.

I decree that backsliding has served its time in my life. Hypocrisy no longer has a place in my life because I possess all the qualities and traits of Jesus. I am no longer ruthless, selfish, or immature in my thinking or behaviors.

God, I know that who I was before has offended you and others at some point. I ask that you forgive me and give me the courage and discernment to know who I owe an apology. God, I thank you for making me over and for removing all the residue from my past.

In Jesus' name, I pray. Amen.

I've Been Thinking

Trust in the Lord with all thine heart; and lean not unto thine own understanding.
Proverbs 3:5 (KJV)

God, I have been thinking way too much! I overthink and analyze a lot of things – please help me to stop. Overthinking has prevented me from accomplishing things I am fully capable of achieving. The things I did achieve took me years when it could have taken me hours if only I put my trust in you.

God, I believe that you have placed certain things in my heart and on my mind for a reason. I will lean on you to help me see them through. God, I acknowledge that you hold all power. I know that you are directing my path as you said in Proverbs 3:6.

Forgive me for allowing my thinking to overshadow your thoughts. Allow me to experience peace of mind and release the weight and pressure I often place upon myself. I pray for wisdom and knowledge to take over when I revert to my understanding instead of yours.

Today, I will trust you! I will acknowledge you in all my ways and wait for your glory to be revealed.

In Jesus' name, I pray. Amen.

Somehow, Some Way

Jesus looked at them and said, "With man this is impossible, but with God all things are possible."
Matthew 19:26 (NIV)

Trusting someone is not an easy thing to do when I feel let me down by them. God, I believe that you exist, but sometimes it is difficult for me to trust you. I have experienced many curve balls and what seems to be unanswered prayers. It is only difficult to yield to you at times because I do not fully understand your logic on things.

Even though it is difficult to trust you, I do. I know that all the pain I go through is preparing me for my gain. When I think about life's hardest moments, I realize that you were the glue that held me together.

Somehow you kept me strong when I was ready to let go. Some way you came to my rescue when I got myself in trouble. Somehow you cared for me when I doubted your ability to be God. Some way you allowed me to meet someone to stay in my corner even when I tried to force them away.

Somehow you are better to me than I am to myself. I commit to being better to you trusting that somehow and some way you will always see me through. God, I believe that nothing is impossible with you.

In Jesus' name, I pray. Amen.

1 Am Healed

O Lord my God, I cried unto thee, and thou hast healed me.
Psalm 30:2 (KJV)

Jesus, Jesus, Jesus, I am calling on your name so that I can be healed. Heal my body so that it can function in the way that you created it to operate. Remove all the pain and symptoms that have come over me. Heal my organs, cells, and vital body parts. Heal me from all diseases, sickness, and infections.

Heal all of me inside and out. Heal everything the doctor diagnosed and the things they did not. Heal all the areas in my body that have altered due to stress. Heal my mind and spirit so that I can have rest. Heal me from migraines, pain, and the destruction of sin in Jesus' name.

In Matthew 4:4, you said that man shall not live on bread alone but on every word, that comes from the mouth of God. I will read your word because I trust that it will bring healing to my life. Your word is the substance I need to live. Help me to speak only your word so that I can see what I say manifest in my situation.

In Jesus' name, I pray. Amen.

Use Me

Behold, I am the Lord, the God of all flesh: is there anything too hard for me?
Jeremiah 32:27 (KJV)

I am a sinner who your grace saves every day. I am forgiven for my unbelief and doubt in you. I am delivered from selfishness and pride that hinders me from being available to you. Today, I am back in business and ask that you use me.

The curse that the enemy had over my life is destroyed. I no longer have a spirit of fear but of power, love, and a sound mind. No weapon that forms against me, my family, church, and job shall prosper. Your hand is on me, and the enemy cannot harm me.

I refuse to be burdened by the lack of trust that I chose to give you because I am moving forward. I am free from ungodly friends, thoughts, and desires. I am free from putting more physical, spiritual, and mental time into things of the world. I am intentional about renewing my mind, and I expect to be transformed as it says in Romans 12:2.

I am committed to indulging in your word so that I know your expectations of me. I decree that I have a consistent and deep relationship with you. I can hear your voice clearly speaking to me, and I will do what you say.

You can use me, God! Nothing that I am or nothing that I will go through disqualifies me from being a vessel to bring you glory. I am entirely selfless and submissive to you, and what you call me to do, I will do.

In Jesus' name, I pray. Amen.

I Cheated

Be not deceived; God is not mocked: for whatsoever a man soweth, that shall he also reap.
Galatians 6:7 (KJV)

God, I messed up. I hurt a person who truly loves and cares about me by acting irrational. I know I deserve everything coming to me. I just pray that you will extend your mercy to me again.

Hebrews 4:16 says that if I come boldly to you, I may receive mercy and find grace in my time of need. Today is my time of need. I need to be cleansed from the inside out. I want to have control over my thoughts, retaliation, and behaviors. Make me into a better person.

I feel bad for what I did, but I am afraid it will happen again. I pray that you remove my lustful desire to have anyone other than the spouse you created for me.

Strengthen me to say no and to walk away from compromising situations. Give me a spirit to discern who to engage with and who to let go. Remove me from toxic environments where the spirit of sexual sin freely roams.

Help me not to be insensitive to the hurt I have caused those who trusted me to be the person I proclaimed to be. Heal their hearts.

Today, I claim freedom and forgiveness because of your love and mercy towards me. Today, I forgive myself and make it my business to do right by you and others.

In Jesus' name, I pray. Amen.

Be Confident

Being confident of this very thing, that he which hath begun a good work in you will perform it until the day of Jesus Christ.
Philippians 1:6 (KJV)

Today no matter what things result in, I will be focused on the bigger picture. I know that things are not happening to me, but for me to fulfill my purpose.

God, I am confident in your ability to lead and guide me. I can feel my confidence improving, and it is making life easier. I will continue to have pure and positive thoughts towards myself to the point where negativity cannot exist.

It is confidence that will cut through my fears and doubts. Courage will keep me excited for what is to come. My confidence will carry me into the next dimension of faith. Allow my confidence to silence negativity caused by my self-doubt.

Today, I choose to put on confidence and wear it daily. I choose to live in assurance and expectation for greatness, favor, and grace. I am confident that what you have begun in me will be completed.

In Jesus' name, I pray. Amen.

I'm Ready for It

Be always on the watch, and pray that you may be able to escape all that is about to happen, and that you may be able to stand before the Son of Man.
Luke 21:36 (NIV)

Today I will have the mind and heart of Christ. I will have a righteous walk, talk, attitude, and overall character! I do not question you, God. I trust, accept, and will easily adapt to the path you have for my life. I will fulfill my purpose. I will focus on the vision that you have given me.

Nothing that comes my way will have the power to knock me off my battlefield because prayer is my armor. God give me the victory as you get the glory. Whatever is to come I ask you to prepare me for it. Provide a place of protection for my family and me in the midst.

I refuse to lose my hope, peace, joy, or faith in you. I declare that will have all that I need regardless of the curve balls thrown at me. I am overflowing with wisdom, knowledge, and understanding. I will remain confident and secure.

I have an abundance of great health and wealth with plenty of storage! I have the power and the spirit of you living inside me, and it will lead, guide, and protect me forever.

In Jesus' name, I pray. Amen.

Dance in the Rain

To everything there is a season, and a time to every
purpose under the heaven.
Ecclesiastes 3:1 (KJV)

God, you will not put more on me than I can bear. I believe
that you created me for a time such as this. Your word says
that nothing is new under the sun. It says that there is a time
to die, mourn, weep, lose, war, and even a time to refrain
from embracing change.

It is your word that validates the war in my mind and my
feelings at this moment. You understand what I am going
through and what it will take for me to make it through. Your
word says that there will be a time to heal, laugh, dance, be
down, and built back up. I am ready for my re-building. I
may never understand what has caused the events in my life
to occur, but I believe that you do not make mistakes.

Make me the rock to stand firm for my family and be my rock
in my time of weakness. Give me the courage to dance while
it rains for I know that the sun will soon shine again.

When the sun shines this time, I pray that it shines over the
devil's parade leaving him no choice but to run and hide
away from me.

In Jesus' name, I pray. Amen.

Share the Goodness

Instead, you must worship Christ as Lord of your life. And if someone asks about your hope as a believer, always be ready to explain it.
1 Peter 3:15 (NLT)

God, you are enough! You make me happy, and you are always looking out for me. Your sense of humor is refreshing. Your faithfulness to me is unmatched. I love you for what you do in my life but mostly for who you are to me. You are forgiving, caring, and you love me more than anyone in the world.

You know just what to say, just what doors to open, and which ones to close. It is amazing to know that nothing can ever stop you from loving me according to Romans 8. You intentionally created me unique so that I would not have to worry about comparing myself to others.

I thank you for waking me up today. I still have life in my body that means my work is not done. Help me to be bolder in my faith. I no longer want to be secretive about your goodness. I ask that you give me the words to say to help others share in your goodness.

Allow the joy and peace that I have to resonate in my relationship with others. Help me to lead others to you when they come to me for advice and encouragement. I am confident that the same way you care about me you care about them. Help them to see that their hope is in you.

In Jesus' name, I pray. Amen.

Nothing Left to Say

In the same way, the Spirit helps us in our weakness. We do not know what we ought to pray for, but the Spirit himself intercedes for us through wordless groans.
Romans 8:26 (NIV)

Today is one of the days where I am just tired. I am exhausted. I am overwhelmed I cannot even think of what tomorrow may bring. By faith, I believe that nothing just happens because you have a divine purpose for my life.

I have given so much of myself to others that I have nothing left for me. I ask that you fill me with your Spirit today. As I pray to you, allow your Spirit to speak on behalf of my silence. I do not know what to pray or even ask of you other than to lead me. Fill every void in my life with your Spirit.

Regardless of what happens I just pray that you allow me to keep my spirit of gratitude. God, I thank you for blessing me and providing me with things I never knew I needed. Thank you for all the ways you make that I do not even realize is your doing.

I decree that new strength is coming to me today. I thank you for the fresh anointing and joy that is being outwardly reflected in my life today. I thank you for hearing my heart even when my mind ignores it. I love you, and I thank you.

In Jesus' name, I pray. Amen.

Failure Proof

*The LORD says, I will guide you along the best pathway
for your life. I will advise you and watch over you.*
Psalm 32:8 (NLT)

I am nor will I ever be a failure. I have failed many times, but
my record of failings does not define the course of my life.
Today, I will follow the guidance and advice from you,
knowing that you will lead me into prosperity.

God, I make you my life coach and ask that you continue to
work with me. You are loving and gentle, so I know that you
will not override my ability to do the things I choose to do.
Today I will obey you, follow, and leave behind the things
and people that do not fit on the pathway to my purpose.

With you failure is not an option. You will not leave or
forsake me as it says in Deuteronomy 31:6. If I choose to go
then that is on me, but because you are merciful, you will
continue watching over me. God help me to not take for
granted your mercy and my ability in you to be failure proof.
I want to remain humble and not be arrogant because I live in
your favor, grace, and mercy.

I know that without you I would be a failure and bouncing
back from failing would be much harder to do. I praise you
for walking and talking me through life. Thank you for
securing my success so that failure has no place in my life.

In Jesus' name, I pray. Amen.

Prepare Me to Parent

Train up a child in the way he should go: and when he is old, he will not depart from it.
Proverbs 22:6 (KJV)

God prepare me to be the best parent for my child and future children. Prepare me with the right amount of patience, sensitivity, warmth, compassion, discipline, and love. Fill me with your wisdom, knowledge, and understanding so that I can help usher them into their destiny ordained by you.

I want to protect them from experiencing some things I did. I know that having a child is not my opportunity for a do-over in my life. Remove the worry, anxiety, and fear I have about my past being repeated in my child's life. I know that whatever I sow, I will reap as it reads in Galatians 6:7. Help me to plant good things.

When you begin to speak to my child give me the strength to remove my opinions. I just ask that you give me your Spirit so I can teach, guide, and offer the advice you want me to give. Make me a praying, dependable, sacrificial, and trustworthy parent. God, you provide for me so I refuse to worry about how my child's needs will be met. I know you have a plan.

I want to instill good morals into my child some which I may or may not possess myself. God where I lack step in so that my inability does not affect my child.

In Jesus' name, I pray. Amen.

No Prayer, No Power | Amber R. Morson

Satisfying Sin

The temptations in your life are no different from what others experience. And God is faithful. He will not allow the temptation to be more than you can stand. When you are tempted, he will show you a way out so that you can endure.
1 Corinthians 10:13 (NLT)

Sometimes sin feels right, it is fun, and seems to release my stress. Sometimes I do not see anything wrong with the things that I do because nothing bad is coming from it. I know I should not have this mentality because sin no matter how it makes me feel disappoints you. God, I know that the devil is strategic, he wants me right where he has me – being satisfied in my sin.

I know what I need to do to be better the hardest part is just doing something about it. God help me to see that I cannot do it without you. Help me to take the way of escape that you provide. Do not allow me to succumb to satisfying sin. I want you to be pleased with me. It is one thing to disappoint myself but another to keep disappointing you.

God, I need your power to release me from the bondage of satisfying sin. Be with me and keep me.

In Jesus' name, I pray. Amen.

Bit by a Bug

Be not deceived: evil communications corrupt good manners.
1 Corinthians 15:33 (KJV)

God, I have lost myself, and the people that know me best do not even recognize me. Help me to find who I was before. At times I am angry, short-tempered, lustful, bitter, selfish, and the things that I say and do hurt people.

You warned me about giving a foot to the enemy in Ephesians 4:27 and now it seems like he has a mile. Forgive me for not taking your word seriously. God, I have been bitten by a dangerous bug. Please be the repellant that blocks the enemy from biting my mind and spirit again.

God if it is distasteful communication that has corrupted my character teach me how to tune it out. If its contact with people who vent to me, music, the news, or anything else that has led me to this place release it.

Today prayer is what will bring back my God-given character.

Today, I will be more watchful about the conversations I have. I will go the extra mile to protect my character, morals, and motives. I will hold positive conversations with everyone on purpose, not only so I can be freed but so they can too.

In Jesus' name, I pray. Amen.

Chance Changed Me

And Philip said, If thou believest with all thine heart, thou mayest. And he answered and said, I believe that Jesus Christ is the Son of God.
Acts 8:37 (KJV)

God, you are so amazing! I took a chance on trusting in your word, and you came through. I believe that Jesus Christ is your son and I will not allow the cares of life to make me think otherwise. My mind is forever changed. It is a blessing to know I am covered by the blood of Jesus.

In my mind, when I took a chance and put my faith in you, I knew that there was a possibility that I could fail. It is crazy looking back on how I approached my relationship with you - cautious, timid, and uncertain. Now, I know that you are exactly who you claim to be. I now know that in you I live and have my being as it says in Acts 17:28.

I am grateful for the things that you did not do when you had reason to. When I consciously disobeyed you, mistreated your people, and made decisions that could have cost me my life, your goodness and mercy covered me.

God, I will always put my faith in you! I love you, and I thank you for giving me another chance to experience your goodness.

In Jesus' name, I pray. Amen.

Tough Call

For all have sinned, and come short of the glory of God.
Romans 3:23 (KJV)

God, I made what looked like the best decision for me. Now I sometimes regret it not knowing if I made the right decision. People make me feel like you would be more pleased with me if I had chosen another way.

I am not perfect! Help me to see that everyone makes extremely tough decisions at some point in life. I can live with not knowing whether I made the right call, but I do not want the "what ifs" being replayed in my mind and heart. Give me peace in my decision because no matter what I know that you love me.

God, release, reset, and recharge me as I move on. I am ready for the next tough call because this time I will let you call the shots and they will work in my favor.

In Jesus' name, I pray. Amen.

Authority in Me

One day Jesus called together his twelve disciples and gave them power and authority to cast out all demons and to heal all diseases.
Luke 9:1 (NLT)

God, I am sick of the devil having power over my family, messing with our minds, finances, and character! It stops today. You have given me the authority to walk over the enemy – so I know that he is powerlessly under my feet. Today, I intercede on behalf of my family because I know that prayer is the only thing that will help us.

Satan, I rebuke you in the name of Jesus and cast you back to the pits of hell from which you came. I command you to leave my bloodline born and yet to be born alone. God has given me the spirit of power, and I am not scared of you and your diminishing tactics. Today, your time has come to an end.

Forgive us God for the role we played in letting the devil take over our family. Prepare me to be the best example for my family of what surrendering to you can do.

I decree and declare that my bloodline is overflowing with grace, mercy, and freedom. We are free from all generational curses. I decree that my family is overcoming addictions and strongholds today! Today we have been set free from the cage of sin. I beseech victory, power, and deliverance to remain in my bloodline forever.

In Jesus' name, I pray. Amen.

No Payback

Touch not mine anointed, and do my prophets no harm.
Psalm 105:15 (KJV)

The problems I am going through right now are only temporary. God take my hands and heart out of the situation. Restrain me from retaliating. Lord, keep me in my place for my place is not to do your job. You have me covered and are better equipped to handle this situation.

It is not my responsibility to respond to nonsense. In Matthew 5:44, it says that I should love and pray for those who persecute me, so here I am. I am praying that you forgive them for they know not what they did. Help me to be slow to anger and pettiness so that I will not sin against you while trying to take up for myself.

I know who I am, I know whose I am, and I know who I serve. You are Lord over my life, and I know that you will not let rumors, truth, and lies shared by hateful people harm me. I refuse to stoop down to a level I have already surpassed.

In Jesus' name, I pray. Amen.

Good Representation

No one lights a lamp and hides it in a clay jar or puts it under a bed. Instead, they put it on a stand, so that those who come in can see the light.
Luke 8:16 (NIV)

God, help my light to shine. It is not a secret that I believe in you, but sometimes I wonder if my life reflects who you are to me. I am not pleased with where I have you prioritized in my life. I do not want you to deny me in heaven for hiding who you are to me here on earth as you said in Matthew 10:33.

Today I will be a better representation of you. Cause my light to shine where ever I go. Change me so that I am a suitable public display of your unconditional love. Change my interactions, conversations, and behaviors to reflect your goodness.

Help me to rejoice when everything about my situation says I should be angry. When others are anticipating my fall, keep me elevated with a level of strength that surpasses all understanding. Fix my faith in areas where it is weak.

I want to take the calling you have over my life seriously. I want others to experience your favor just for being connected to me. All the areas in my life where darkness hides reveal it so I can be a better use for your glory.

In Jesus' name, I pray. Amen.

God Can

For we are his workmanship, created in Christ Jesus unto good works, which God hath before ordained that we should walk in them.
Ephesians 2:10 (KJV)

God, you warned me not to get weary in well doing. I am unsure of what to do because I am tired. I have followed what seemed to be the right path. I am a hardworking and honest person with dignity.

God, I have an opportunity of a lifetime in my reach, and I know that it is because of you. God, make way for me to do what I can and what I cannot do, you will do. I am not the most educated, skilled, professional, or worthy person fit for an opportunity like this, but you can qualify me. You can speak highly about me to the people my voice will never reach and cause them to advocate on my behalf.

God, I believe that you can do this and I pray that you will. You can create the doors that no man can shut. Give me confidence in the contentment I feel when I turn things over to you. I will not stress or overthink this opportunity because I cannot control the outcome only you can. I decree that victory is mine.

In Jesus' name, I pray. Amen.

My Strength

This is what the Lord says: "Cursed are those who put their trust in mere humans, who rely on human strength and turn their hearts away from the Lord."
Jeremiah 17:5 (NLT)

God, thank you for making me a strong person. Being strong has been both a blessing and a curse. It is a blessing because life does not defeat me. It is a curse because I think I can handle everything on my on.

As a strong individual, I do not like to show weakness. However, it is weak to rely only on my strength and not be vulnerable enough to rely on yours.

I am accustomed to being the "strong one." I keep my needs bottled up inside. I am tired of pretending like I am good when I know I am not. Give me your strength because mine is failing.

Teach me to decipher between my strength and your strength. Drive out my desire to lean on me and not you. Today, I put my trust back in you. I trust that all my help will come from you as it says in Psalms 121.

In Jesus' name, I pray. Amen.

Seasonal Situations

And he changeth the times and the seasons: he removeth kings, and setteth up kings: he giveth wisdom unto the wise, and knowledge to them that know understanding.
Daniel 2:21 (KJV)

No matter what happens in life, I believe that you want what is best for me. God, the seasons in my life are only situations, and I declare that the result will reflect you. Nothing that I lost last year or will lose this year will hinder me from fulfilling the script you wrote for my life.

Help me to be confident in your decision to change my script and remove things from it. For I know that what you eliminate you will replace. I declare that this scene I am in is not what it appears to be. I declare that after I have suffered a while, God you will restore me as it says in 1 Peter 5:10.

God use my seasonal situations to grow me and to teach me. Give me the wisdom to take heed to all of the intended lessons. I pray for stronger faith, endurance, and a greater testimony after each season. I decree that I will not get stuck in any season you have called me to come out of.

In Jesus' name, I pray. Amen.

Patience is Key

Patient endurance is what you need now, so that you will continue to do God's will. Then you will receive all that he has promised.
Hebrew 10:36 (NLT)

Today I am going to celebrate the renewed patience that is coming to me. By faith I claim the endurance and maturity to wait it out with ease. Last year, I was impatient and overwhelmed by the things I wanted right away. God your word instructs me to have patience as I endurance.

You never promised that the wait would be easy. I pray that you help me to be a good waiter - a server. Teach me to be attentive and timely as I wait on you. After my waiting is over, I know that I will receive all that you promised.

It is no secret that the best waiter often gets the best tip, mold me into the best waiter. Help me to recall all the things you asked of me so that I can be sure to do them. Do not let me quit when the demands are high for Galatians 6:9 says that I will reap in due season if I do not give up.

I will wait on you and move when you tell me to.

In Jesus' name, I pray. Amen.

New Opportunities

For everything there is a season, a time for every activity
under heaven.
Ecclesiastes 3:1 (NLT)

God, I just want to thank you today. Thank you for giving me something new just when being content was plaguing my life. You heard my silent cry for a new and exciting venture, and you provided it.

With this new opportunity, I pray that you bring a newness of joy, influence, and peace. Help me to make a positive impact in the life of someone else. At times when I may feel nervous or not prepared lead me. Help me to bask in the growth and adventure this new opportunity will bring.

Growth and adventure bring forth change, and I want to embrace the change. Help me to not be fearful at the site of change because of how change negatively impacted my past. I declare that this is a change in the right direction.

In Jesus' name, I pray. Amen.

Stop Judging

The standard you use in judging is the standard by which you will be judged.
Matthew 7:2 (NLT)

God, forgive me for being a judgmental Christian and forgive people for judging me. I do not know where in the bible it says that as a Christian I am to be nothing but perfect. People place Christians on such a high pedestal when it should be you held up there.

God, I thank you for the life I live. I enjoy my life, my family, and friends. I love being a recipient of your grace and mercy. Everyone will not understand my relationship with you, and I will not understand yours with them. Instead of judging ground me and my thoughts in love and compassion.

God, I have judged people unfairly before, and I pray that you forgive me. Help me instead to see people for who they are whether that be good or bad. Help me to judge only in comparison to your word, not my opinion.

In Jesus' name, I pray. Amen.

Cover My Leadership

For we are not fighting against flesh-and-blood enemies,
but against evil rulers and authorities of the unseen world,
against mighty powers in this dark world, and against evil
spirits in the heavenly places.
Ephesians 6:12 (NLT)

My prayer today is that you cover all people in leadership positions throughout the world. Much pressure comes with being a leader. Although I may not understand everything that goes on behind the scenes – you do.

Not all leaders are good; some are wicked with evil spirits and motives. However, your power is far greater than any evil spirit or unruly authority. I pray that you eliminate the barriers set up against good leaders. Keep them grounded as they fight through daily attacks and lies people may bring their way. I rebuke the spirit of suicide, fear, and failure that have overtaken so many leaders today.

I pray that you elevate more God-fearing people into leadership positions. Give them the tools they need to be successful and to inspire success in others. In Proverbs 16:7 it says that when our ways please you, you will cause peace between our enemies and us.

God send the peace. Bring forth the elevation of new leadership. Cover the present leaders and protect them.

In Jesus' name, I pray. Amen.

Crucial Conversations

*Don't use foul or abusive language. Let everything you say
be good and helpful, so that your words will be an
encouragement to those who hear them.*
Ephesians 4:29 (NLT)

Today, I am praying for the courage to have a conversation I
should have had a long time ago. I feel like I will be much
better without this situation weighing on my conscience. I
pray that I do not get nervous or catch an attitude, which
could lead this conversation down the wrong path.

Instead, I ask that you give me the words to say, allow my
words to be constructive instead of detrimental. God, before I
have this talk remove any bitterness or resentment in my
heart. God, release any hidden motives I might have going
into this conversation and reveal if they have any.

I pray that I remain true to who I am and be completely
honest with myself and the other person. Please, God, do not
allow me to shut down, be bamboozled, or overpowered.
Grace me with your attentive thoughts so that I can listen for
understanding and not to rebuttal what is said.

By faith, I know that you are with me and will protect me as I
have this crucial conversation. In the end, I pray that I feel
better and end up in a place where I am free from worry and
wonder.

In Jesus' name, I pray. Amen.

Forgive and Forget

Be kind and compassionate to one another, forgiving each other, just as in Christ God forgave you.
Ephesians 4:32 (NIV)

God, teach me how to forgive and forget. My mindset has always been to forgive others but not forget how they made me feel or what they did. It is like I forgive, but then I keep a detailed rap sheet of every person who did me wrong. Whenever I try to forget and forgive people, it seems like as soon as they mess up again, all the memories come back from the past.

Matthew 6:15 says that if I do not forgive others, you would not forgive me, so I am praying for direction on how to properly forgive others and myself. I know that when you forgive me for my sins, you give me a clean slate, never holding my past against me. My prayer is that I learn to forgive and forget in the same manner as you.

I decree by faith that from now on I will view forgiveness in a new way. Forgiveness is not for the other person, but it is for me. I decree that I will forgive because I am forgiven. Make me quick to forgive so that I do not carry the weight of bitterness, rage, and anger around with me.

Free my heart from all the unforgiveness inside and fill it up with the same love and compassion you give to me every time I mess up.

In Jesus' name, I pray. Amen.

I Won't be Defeated

Many are the afflictions of the righteous, but the Lord delivers him out of them all.
Psalms 34:19 (KJV)

Sometimes life takes a toll on my confidence. I get overwhelmed, stressed, and tired of dealing with all the ups and downs. I know that you have made me special and the trials that come my way are not too big for me to defeat.

I am grateful to know that I will never have to go through pain and suffer alone. God, I know you are on my side as it says in Psalms 118 so I will not fear. Fear of the unknown defeats so many people and I pray you keep me from being one of them. I pray that trusting you becomes simpler for me.

Help me to view trusting you as the prerequisite for overcoming all trouble. I know that as I trust you things will be better for me in the end. Today, I am going to make a conscious decision to trust you. I decree and declare that I will not let the concerns of today defeat my spirit and steal my joy.

I will not be defeated because I have the undefeated champ of this world fighting alongside me.

In Jesus' name, I pray. Amen.

Distract my Distractions

Look straight ahead, and fix your eyes on what lies before you.
Proverbs 4:25 (NLT)

God, my prayer today is that you help me to focus. I get distracted so easily by my phone, social media, video games, food, sleep, people, etc. I do not understand why I allow these things to take my attention away from specific things I set out to accomplish.

I feel like I should be involved in everything that catches my attention. This mindset has only aided in me being distracted even more. Teach me to keep my mind on what I need to be doing. I have been excusing my distractions by calling them multi-tasking. Your word instructs me to fix my eyes on what is ahead of me, and I pray for help in this area.

Fix means to secure something in a specific place or position. I pray that you position me in a place where the things that distract me are not present. Help me to determine a focus area where I can go and be distraction free.

Today, I am going to seek out that place intentionally. I am going to work on being present and engaged in things without giving half of myself to it.

In Jesus' name, I pray. Amen.

The Best Man

In all things shewing thyself a pattern of good works: in doctrine shewing uncorruptness, gravity, sincerity.
Titus 2:7 (KJV)

God, there is an attack on manhood and no one can do anything about it but you. God raise up bold, secure, and honest men to be the example of what a true man of God is. Many people claim to want a man of God and believe that they are one – but do not even know you.

Matthew 7 says that I will know if people are false by the fruit that they bare. God give me discernment to know which men to consider as a friend, mentor, or for guidance based on their actions.

A man of God has a track record of being and doing good unto others. They are men who exercise self-control as it says in Titus 2:2. They exude patience, and they are filled with love!

The world has tried to make men believe that they were created to be hardcore, savages with little to no care, or concern about others – the devil is a liar! Raise up men to love. Help them to love themselves and others freely and sincerely.

God, please cover all the men in my life with your protection.

In Jesus' name, I pray. Amen.

Fix My Priorities

But seek ye first the kingdom of God, and his righteousness; and all these things shall be added unto you.
Matthew 6:33 (KJV)

God, please help me to get my life together. I have so many things on my mind about finances, health, and safety all while trying to be successful and enjoy life. Help me to reprioritize! In all honesty, our relationship gets shifted on my priority list more than anything else. Forgive me!

Help me to refocus and reframe the way I set my priorities. God, I believe that when I seek you first and aim to live right by you everything else will fall in line. Paint the picture of what seeking you first actually looks like for my life.

I work hard to set myself up to be in a position where I can get the things I want out of life. I often fail to realize that you are the supplier of everything I can ever want or need. When my priorities are in their proper place, I have fewer worries and anxiety.

God, I repent for trying to outdo you and labeling it as hustling and grinding. I decree and declare that my priorities will remain in order. I decree and declare that when my life is in order, I will be in the best position to be blessed.

In Jesus' name, I pray. Amen.

Every Day Matters

The thief cometh not, but for to steal, and to kill, and to destroy: I am come that they might have life, and that they might have it more abundantly.
John 10:10 (KJV)

God, today I just want to confess that my belief and hope is in you. Although things do not always work out in ways I understand, I know you have good intentions. You said in John 10 that you come that I might have life more abundantly – this lets me know that things will get better.

God, you are mighty, and I know that you love me. You have the power to change my days around. The devil is the only one who wants to steal, kill, and destroy my life, family, relationships, and mind. I pray that all of the things the devil had taken be return tenfold.

God help me to see that if I am alive, it is my responsibility to live! This year I am going to live expecting every day to get better than before. I am reclaiming my joy, my hope, and restoring my trust in you today!

I will not allow the devil's deception to cause me to take my life. I decree that I will live to tell everyone how you have made every day matter for me.

In Jesus' name, I pray. Amen.

The Cost of Faith

I have been crucified with Christ and I no longer live, but Christ lives in me. The life I now live in the body, I live by faith in the Son of God, who loved me and gave himself for me.
Galatians 2:20 (NIV)

I use the word faith so freely, but I often wonder if my faith is working. Faith is simply believing or having assurance in hope without present evidence. James 2:17 says that faith without works is dead and I think that working should cost me something. Naturally, when I work, it cost me my time, energy, and it may even require me to give up my opinion at times. I cannot help but to think that my faith should operate the same way.

Living by faith should cost me to believe beyond my current circumstances. It should cost me giving up bad habits and stagnant thinking. It should cost me believing that your ways are better than my own. Help me to act in ways that will activate my faith.

My prayer is that I exude the type of faith that allows you to live out your life through mine freely. God, you died so that the only cost of grace, mercy, and favor to me is my faith in your son Jesus.

I pray that you help me to see that Jesus paid the price for my faith, my job is only to believe. Fill me with faith and faithfulness because I do not just want to have faith, but I want to be faithful to you.

In Jesus' name, I pray. Amen.

No Prayer, No Power | Amber R. Morson

Do Your Job

But I say unto you, love your enemies, bless them that
curse you, do good to them that hate you, and pray for
them which despitefully use you, and persecute you.
Matthew 5:44 (KJV)

God, forgive me for crossing the line as I have fought, hated, and dismissed people who have done me wrong. That never has and will never be my job – my job is to love, bless, and pray for them. When people do me or others wrong, help me to watch what I say about them. Rid me of my nature to gossip. Take away the satisfaction that gossiping brings me. Give me the strength to be better and not to be bitter.

Loving those who are selfish and rude has nothing to do with me but everything to do with me pleasing you. I know that you instructed me to pray for those who persecute me for a reason. I trust your reasoning. I pray that you teach me to bless and release people from my life without having anger in my heart.

God, every time that I bless someone who does not want to see me blessed, bless me double! Change my attitude and perspective on troublesome people. I pray that you bless me with the humility and courage to pray for them. I pray that every time I do good unto a problematic person, you will do good unto me.

In Jesus' name, I pray. Amen.

Stretch Me

*Then the Lord said to Moses, "Stretch out your hand over
the sea so that the waters may flow back over the
Egyptians and their chariots and horsemen."*
Exodus 14:26 (NIV)

Today I pray that you will stretch me in every area of my life.
Stretch me in my giving, praying, work ethic, in my level of
dedication, and consistency. Stretch me until I am completely
relieved of all things, not like you.

As I stretch, I declare that joy, peace, and broken
relationships are restored in my life. As I stretch, I trust that
you will make everything broken in me whole again. I pray
that my stretching is the warm-up I need to make it to a
higher level of faith. I pray that my faith becomes so flexible
that trusting you in all things becomes easier than the day
before.

God, I declare that I will become stronger after I allow you to
stretch me. I will become healthier after I reach beyond my
poor habits. I will be wiser, better, and more courageous after
I extend my effort. Give me a desire to stretch my faith so
when my usual reaction is to shrink I become so
uncomfortable that my comfort will only be found when I
stretch my faith.

In Jesus' name, I pray. Amen.

Elevator Haters

And ye shall be hated of all men for my name's sake: but he
that endureth to the end shall be saved.
Matthew 10:22 (KJV)

God help me to shift my thinking when it comes to those that hate on me. People always say that your haters will be your elevators. I cannot help but to think about how elevators go up and down. My prayer is that you would help me during the times when my haters are pulling me down. Help me to endure when I am being pulled down!

The good thing about elevators is that they have limitations. They are not built to take me any lower than the engineer designed them to go. God, you are the engineer of my life. You will not allow anyone or anything to drag me to a point so low I cannot rise from it.

Today, I am not going to complain about the haters; I am going to say thank you. Today, I pray that when I am being pulled down, I will fly higher like a bow and arrow. God, help me to endure all the hate for your name's sake.

In Jesus' name, I pray. Amen.

Bold Believers

Boldly proclaiming the Kingdom of God and teaching about the Lord Jesus Christ. And no one tried to stop him.
Acts 28:31 (NLT)

God, sometimes I can be a timid believer. Too afraid to have faith concerning more significant issues in my life because eventually, my mind tells me to "be realistic." As if you, your grace, mercy, and favor are not real. If all it takes for me to stop having faith is doubt, I need to reconsider whose I am.

God, cause the eyes of my understanding to be enlightened so that I may know what riches are to be inherited as it says in Ephesians 1:18. Make me allergic to timidness, and help me to only find comfort in being a bold believer!

I will no longer think my way out of a blessing. I will no longer think my way out of what you have called me to be. You called me to talk about who you are with boldness. I declare that as I boldly profess you will boldly bless.

In Jesus' name, I pray. Amen.

No Prayer, No Power | Amber R. Morson

Live the Legacy

Praise ye the Lord. Blessed is the man that feareth the Lord, that delighteth greatly in his commandments. His seed shall be mighty upon earth: the generation of the upright shall be blessed.
Psalm 112:1-2 (KJV)

Many people are concerned about having money to leave behind as a legacy for their family. My concern has been similar - be successful in getting ahead for me and my family. My prayer today is that I will live the legacy you want me to leave.

God, you are important to me. I fear you and earnestly strive to follow your commandments. For these reasons, your word says that my seeds shall be mighty upon the earth. My seeds are my children, my family, and those who call me a mentor. You have already reassured me that my seeds will be blessed if I live the legacy that you have laid. I pray that you give me the intelligence to live out my legacy without reinventing the wheel.

I thank you for this revelation, and I will walk in it today. Today is my new start! Today, the legacy will not only be left, but lived through me!

In Jesus' name, I pray. Amen.

The Gray Area

Their loyalty is divided between God and the world, and they are unstable in everything they do.
James 1:8 (NLT)

Today is the last day that I will allow gray areas to take up space in my life. The drunkenness, the habitual sin, the lying, the idols, the cheating, the scamming, and the jealousy – it all ends today! I am sick of having one foot in and one foot out. I am smart enough to know right from wrong, and I decree that I am strong enough to live right.

God, I never want to offend you by being more loyal to my family, spouse, job, or even school than I am to you. I am entirely faithful to many things in my life, no matter what, right or wrong. You deserve the same unwavering love and loyalty from me.

I want stability to rest in my life, and my loyalty to you is what will provide it. I no longer want to be easily persuaded to sin "just this one time" because although it may not hurt me, I know that it bothers you. Free me of any gray areas in life known and unknown.

In Jesus' name, I pray. Amen.

Jesus Did It

Now unto him that is able to do exceeding abundantly
above all that we ask or think, according to the power
that worketh in us.
Ephesians 3:20 (KJV)

Thank you, Jesus, for loving me. I wish I could wrap my head around why you love me so much. I am so grateful that you see fit to protect me. You love me enough to bless me when I do not even deserve it. You continue to provide for me when I think the ends will not be met. You always have my back even when I intentionally do not have yours.

You find multiple ways to bless me with things I never thought I needed or could afford. It is refreshing to know that nothing I do can ever separate me from your love as it says in Romans 8. I will forever tell of your goodness and mercy towards me.

I decree that my testimony this year will be "Jesus Did It!" I pray for an unexpected blessing this year! I pray that you will do more than what I am asking in prayer. I pray that you bless me with a new normal.

In Jesus' name, I pray. Amen.

Gated Guilt

If we confess our sins, he is faithful and just to forgive us
our sins, and to cleanse us from all unrighteousness.
1 John 1:9 (KJV)

God, I do not want this feeling anymore. I do not want to feel guilt from any of the things I have done in my life. I am better than I was before, please release me from all guilt. Today, as I repent, I pray that you forgive me, and free me from all guilt and shame.

John 3:17 says that you sent Jesus so that I could be saved and not condemned! You do not condemn me for my sins, so I pray that you help me to stop condemning myself. Hebrews 8:12 says that you will be merciful to my unrighteousness and that my sins you will remember no more. Today I accept the clean slate, I take my do-over, and I will rest in the reset.

I repent for putting others before you. I repent for purposely deceiving others to fulfill my agendas. I repent for taking advantage of your people. I repent for mistreating my parents, authority, and your creations. I repent for mismanaging your money and mistaking it for my own. I confess in my heart the things I am too ashamed to acknowledge out loud.

I thank you for forgiving me, and I accept my freedom from guilt.

In Jesus' name, I pray. Amen.

Misinformed

*Consider what I say, for the Lord will give you
understanding in everything.*
2 Timothy 2:7 (NASB)

God, help me to remember that no one is perfect. I have
encountered people who have misused their influence to lie,
cheat, and rob people. Forgive them, God, for they know not
what they have done. Forgive people who tried to control me
by switching your words to manipulate and condemn me.

I pray that you will lead me to preachers who teach and live
your exact word. Place me in the multitude of good
counselors so that I may have safety as it says in Proverbs
11:14. Help me to filter out any wrong teachings I may have
been taught and adopted as the truth.

Remove habits from me that was picked up by bad influences
in my upbringing. I pray that you will help me to learn you
for myself. I desire to know the truth about who you are and
who you have called me to be.

From now on, I decree that as I read your word, I will have
proper wisdom, knowledge, and understanding of it. I will
apply what I have learned to better my life and the lives of
others.

In Jesus' name, I pray. Amen.

I Can Do It

*That the man of God may be perfect, throughly furnished
unto all good works.*
2 Timothy 3:17 (KJV)

God, I am going to take the risk today! I am just going to go
for it! I will stand on your word in Romans 8 that says I am
more than a conqueror through Christ Jesus. I trust you when
you say that I can do all things through you!

God, direct my path and do not allow me to depend on my
intellectual capabilities. I am seeking you first because in
doing so you promised in Matthew 6:33 that all things will be
added to me.

Be with me as I take this leap today. Do not leave or forsake
me. Bind any hindering spirits that will try to distract me
from trusting you for the impossible today. I will not over
think this and I will not overcomplicate this, I will just go for
it! See me through, God.

In Jesus' name I pray, Amen!

Fill the Voids

My flesh and my heart faileth: but God is the strength of my heart, and my portion for ever.
Psalms 73:26 (KJV)

God as I reflect on Psalms 73:26 I am in awe of you! Life has given me many voids from deaths, losses, and disappointments. I do believe that because you had to endure some pain, I am not exempt. However, Psalms 73:26 reminds me that no matter how many times I fail, you are enough to sustain me for eternity! It says that you are my portion forever.

Forever means eternity! Having someone to be persistent about me in life is a blessing, but at any moment that persistence can end. However, eternity has no ending and no limitations! God, no matter the number of voids I may feel you are enough to fill them forever! No matter how many times my dreams shatter, my heart breaks or disappointments drain me; you will keep me!

Thank you for being more than enough! Thank you for filling the emptiness I feel with your love, joy, and care!

In Jesus' name, I pray. Amen.

Expand My Reach

Jabez cried out to the God of Israel, "Oh, that you would bless me and enlarge my territory! Let your hand be with me, and keep me from harm so that I will be free from pain." And God granted his request.
1 Chronicles 4:10 (NIV)

God, thank you for where you are elevating me to today! I know you are on the verge of moving me past my current circumstances. I believe for something big today! I believe that I am first in line for my biggest blessing yet. I praise you, and I thank you in advance for releasing my blessing.

I decree that my new blessings will reach new heights and new consumers. This blessing will be so big that I have no choice but to trust you to guide me through. Someone is not going to envious and, I might even lose a friend, but I will be protected in Jesus name! My attitude, my ego, and my pride will not consume me for I will remain humble, confident, and faithful!

No matter what happens because of my blessing, I will rejoice and be glad. I will stand firm in knowing that you have prepared me and handpicked me for a time such as today! I call forth my blessing now!

In Jesus' name, I pray. Amen.

Clean House

The mind governed by the flesh is hostile to God; it does not submit to God's law nor can it do so.
Romans 8:7 (NIV)

Thank you, God, for forgiving and forgetting my sins. I have sinned against you by not honoring your desires of me. My prayer for today is that you speak to me and unclutter my mind and spirit. Give me an ear and heart to hear from you. Put me in a space where I can listen and apply what you tell me to do. God, I submit to your law.

Sometimes it is difficult to hear your voice, but I know that if others can listen to you, I can too. I pray that you guard my mind against the tricks of the enemy. Please do not let me lose my witness and do not allow my light to dim because of my disobedience, ignorance, and curiosity. Help me to allow my light to shine brighter than ever before so that others will draw near to you.

Help me to refocus and have patience while you do a new work in me. Help me to remember your goodness and faithfulness towards me! Do not let me get weary in well doing. Place me back in the well-doing and help me to stay!

I know that you have favored me with wisdom, knowledge, and understanding. Make me stronger and bolder in the areas I am weak. Strengthen me! Keep me in your will God through the storms, trials, and test.

In Jesus' name, I pray. Amen.

Hindsight

*Where there is no vision, the people perish: but he that
keepeth the law, happy is he.*
Proverbs 29:18 (KJV)

God, I discovered that someone very close to me that I love
and I know loves me does not support me! They believe that I
would be better off staying where I am. They do not see the
vision that I see for myself, and they do not have the faith
that I have. I value their opinion and their desire to keep me
safe, but I want more.

Help me to view this situation differently so that my
relationship with them does not break. Sometimes we need
people close to us to not believe in us so that our frustrations
can push us closer to fulfilling our purpose.

I pray that you bring me to a place where no one's opinion
matters but yours. I want my faith to grow to the point where
you are the only one I consider talking to before I make a
decision. Nobody has my back like you, and I pray that
understanding this becomes easier.

God, I thank you for the vision you have given me. Today I
will plan, strategize, and work towards it so that what I see
spiritually, can manifest itself in the earth.
In Jesus' name, I pray. Amen.

Thank You

I will praise you, LORD, with all my heart; I will tell of all the marvelous things you have done.
Psalm 9:1 (NLT)

Thank you, God, for traveling mercy! You protect me day in and day out as I commute. Whether I am walking, catching the bus, flying, or the passenger in a car, you have always protected me. Today I just want to thank you for the little things I may often overlook.

I thank you for discounts I did not ask for that allowed me to purchase things for my family. I thank you for the times I have rushed to places, and it seemed like you delayed everything so that I could make it on time. Thank you, for strategically placing and removing people from my life.

I thank you for the GPS that gets me to new destinations. I thank you for household items like my toothbrush and tissue. I do not take for granted having lights, water, heat, and air. I thank you for pens and paper, phones, and computers.

I only want to take some time to thank you for my life and for giving me all I need to maintain it.

In Jesus' name, I pray. Amen.

Don't Beg

I was young and now I am old, yet I have never seen the
righteous forsaken or their children begging bread.
Psalm 37: 25 (NIV)

God, I thank you that today is the last day I will have to beg
anyone for anything! Today is the end of me having to plea
and strategize for things you can give me. God, you hold all
power in your hands. Forgive me for the times I begged
people to do and give me things that I could have asked you
to provide.

I declare that my begging days are over. I claim a new level of
faith today. By faith, I will ask and then receive what it is I
ask for. I will remain righteous so that my children or I will
not have to beg for anything ever again. I thank you for your
promises God, especially the one that says you will never
leave or forsake me.

The worry must flee today. Stress has to leave my life today.
Anxiousness will no longer consume me. Begging is a thing
of my past and will not be present in my future. I declare and
decree that all my needs are met!
In Jesus' name, I pray. Amen.

Release Rest

Come to me, all you who are weary and burdened, and I will give you rest.
Matthew 11:28 (NIV)

God, I am tired! I need you to bring rest into my life right now. I am always on the go and busy fulfilling responsibilities. My mind needs rest. My spirit needs rest. My body needs rest.

Help me to find rest in a restless world that tells me I need to grind day in and day out. I want to be successful, but I also want to maintain my peace and sanity. At times, I wake up tired after not doing anything, tired just at the thought of the things I should do. Help me to find rest in the midst of all my responsibilities.

Create avenues for me to find places, people, and things that bring rest and restoration to my life. I pray that you allow me to see the value and the purpose in creating rest. Today, I decree that my house will be a haven, a place of rest, and relaxation.

I thank you for the rest you are releasing in my life right now.

In Jesus' name, I pray. Amen.

Pain & Pride

Let someone else praise you, and not your own mouth; an outsider, and not your own lips.
Proverbs 27: 2 (NIV)

God, I know that all the talents, skills, knowledge, and understanding that I have, come from you. I believe that I am on my way to being the first in my family to do some ground-breaking things! I appreciate you for entrusting me with the strength to accomplish so much.

However, I struggle with pride sometimes. I do not want to get to a place where my pride leads me to a painful fall. Proverbs 16:18 warns me that pride comes before destruction. Help me to see the difference between pride, my faith, and just being proud of my accomplishments.

I repent for the times where I have used faith as an excuse to have a big ego. I repent for boldly proclaiming to be self-made, acting as if you did nothing for me. I ask that you forgive me for not being humble. Forgive me for not being proud of you and what you have accomplished through me.

God, I want you to get the glory out of my life, and I pray that my pride will not hinder that from happening. Humble me in all areas of my life, for your word says in Proverbs 16:19 that it is better to live humbly and not proud.

In Jesus' name, I pray. Amen.

Lose the "Tude"

A cheerful heart is good medicine, but a crushed spirit dries up the bones.
Proverbs 17:22 (NIV)

Thank you, God, for making me unique! Forgive me for the times when I did not appreciate my uniqueness. Forgive me for the times I changed my attitude to fit the likeness of those around me. God, I believe you have called me to have an attitude of Jesus. Today I want to receive the skill, strength, and courage it is going to take for me to fulfill that calling.

Help me to lose my bad attitude. Help me to drop the attitude of entitlement that makes me treat others less than. Free me from having a pessimistic outlook on life. The prideful attitude that has prevented me from asking for help, I give it up today.

I declare that I will have an attitude of love and unity. I will have an attitude that admits when I am wrong. I will have a contagious attitude of gratitude and patience. I will be slow to react in rage and quick to respond in forgiveness. I declare that my attitude will not prevent me from my purpose. My attitude will usher me into a more fulfilling place in life. I declare that today, my attitude changes for the better.

In Jesus' name, I pray. Amen.

Still Happy

Nay, in all these things we are more than conquerors
through him that loved us.
Romans 8:37 (KJV)

God, I come to celebrate and thank you for the victory you declared over Satan on my behalf! Last year the devil threw his best shots at me, he scored, but he did not win the game. I am happy, and I declare that I will stay happy no matter what happens, no matter who comes or goes. God, I know that my happiness is found in you and I choose to accept it.

Today I am making up in my mind not to worry because you do not get glory from worry. You get glory from my ability to have faith, trusting that you will make everything alright.

Today I shout to Satan, "still happy"! Through losing a loved one - I am still happy. Through all the hell on my job, God you still make me happy. Through all the tears, pain, and backstabbing - I am happy. I am still strong, still breathing, praying, trusting, and my bills are still paid! God, no matter what, I am still and will forever be your child.

I thank you, God! I love and honor you for keeping me happy.

In Jesus' name, I pray. Amen.

I Am Enough

*For God hath not given us the spirit of fear; but of power,
and of love, and of a sound mind.*
2 Timothy 1:7 (KJV)

Today I declare that I am enough! God, I am capable of doing
all the things I thought I could not do. I am more than
deserving of all the things you have for me. I may not be the
best, the brightest, or the headliner but I bring something to
the table that no one else does. I will be confident,
courageous, bold yet humble as I walk in my calling.

Today I declare that self-doubt is a thing of the past. I serve
notice on self-doubt today - you must go! My confidence will
no longer be dependent on others realization of who I am.
God stop all the voices in my head and remove all
insecurities that make me doubt myself and my abilities.

I am intelligent and smart enough to figure things out. I am
strong enough to sacrifice my present for my future. This
year will be the last year I talk myself out of doing something.
I rebuke all hindering spirits that have held me back from
living out my full potential.

God, I am who you say I am. I will be what you called me to
be. I will have what you said is mine. I will tap into my God-
given inheritance. I will walk confidently into every situation
forthcoming because I am enough.

In Jesus' name, I pray. Amen.

Make Me A Resource

And do not forget to do good and to share with others, for with such sacrifices God is pleased.
Hebrews 13:16 (NIV)

God, you are a pleasant counselor, friend, and resource. Anytime I need you; you are always there. My prayer today is that you make me a resource for someone else. I do not want to live a life of selfishness only caring about myself.

I am confident that you placed something in me for me to share with someone else. The trials and test that I have overcome were for me to encourage someone. I do not know who the person is but God you know. Allow our paths to cross during this season and time. Give me the discernment to know who they are.

I commit to praying for this person. I commit to being a genuine resource for this person as you are to me, God. I thank you for entrusting me with this responsibility. I thank you for your guidance and instruction as you use me to help those in need. I thank you in advance for the continuation of blessings you will release to me that will allow me to be a resource for your people.

In Jesus' name, I pray. Amen.

The Villain in the Violence

Do not envy the violent or choose any of their ways.
Proverbs 3:31 (NIV)

God, I first want to thank you for shielding my family and I. So much in the world is happening and my prayer today is for the people responsible for the violence. Whatever is going on in their heart and mind, I pray that you will intervene.

God place simple principles like love and compassion in the minds of people who lack them. Help them to stop, think, and fully understand the outcomes of the decisions they plan to make. God right the wrongs of the criminals, killers, molesters, and all people who cause harm in the lives of others. Forgive them for taking matters into their own hands and not trusting you. Heal them from past hurt, insecurities, drama, trauma, and mental illnesses that cause them to act irrationally.

I rebuke Satan's ability to influence your people. I pray against any jealous, malicious, and careless spirits that plague my city and the world. I pray against any stigmas that cause people to suffer in silence, send help their way.

Forgive me for any time I played the role of a villain perpetuating violence. I repent for being careless in my behavior. Help me to yield all my battles past, present, and future over to you.

In Jesus' name, I pray. Amen.

Better

The end of a matter is better than its beginning, and patience is better than pride.
Ecclesiastes 7:8 (NIV)

No matter what is going on in my life, today I declare that you are making it better! God, I may not see it or feel it near but I know better is here. I declare better in my life, relationships, finances, and health! I thank you, God, for making things better right now.

I will no longer wait for a better report or a better opportunity because I am declaring that it is here – right now. Point me in the right direction and do not let me miss it. Do not allow me to become distracted or attracted to anything other than what is better.

God, thank you for making my heart and mind better. Thank you for making my spouse and children better. God, thank you for making my church and my circle of friends a better support system. Thank you for giving me better strength and endurance.

I declare that I am a better friend, confidant, and listener. I have better intentions and a better drive. I am a better provider and protector over my loved ones. I have a better work ethic, better faith, I pray bigger and better prayers. God, I trust you better. I am fulfilling my purpose better.

I thank you for better! I decree that better will stay in my life.

In Jesus' name, I pray. Amen.

I Deserved It

If we confess our sins, he is faithful and just to forgive us our sins and to cleanse us from all **1 John 1:9 (KJV)** *unrighteousness.*

God, thank you for being a gentle redeemer in my life. I deserve to be dead and gone but God, you truly have your hand on me. I know people who did not survive what you allowed me to escape! God, thank you, no one can protect me as you do. No one can provide, forgive, and gracefully discipline as you do. Your favor is unmatched!

I know I was wrong. I knowingly disobeyed you, but you still looked out for me. Everything that should have happened did not, and it is all because you cared. You believed in me, you trusted me to do better, and be better.

I thank you for my second chance. I magnify you for my clean slate. I confess that I am because you are! I now understand just how much I am God made and not self-made. Forgive me for when I proclaimed to be. You deserve all the glory and honor because you pushed me through the storms to bring me out of them. Thank You. I love you.

In Jesus' name, I pray. Amen.

Remaining Consistent

Let us hold tightly without wavering to the hope we affirm, for God can be trusted to keep his promise.
Hebrews 10:23 (NLT)

Before this obstacle reappeared in my life, I was doing perfectly fine. Now that it is back I am a little concerned. Keep me grounded and rooted in a forward mentality. I thank you for the progress I have made thus far, and I ask that you help me to avoid backtracking.

Who I was back then is not who I am now. God help me to bypass old feelings and poor decision making. I will not waste time overthinking how to get over this hump because it is already beneath me. Today, I will view this obstacle as a compliment. Satan, thank you for valuing me so much that you saw fit to try and attack me with what worked before. I decree and declare - never again!

God keep me consistent in the place I am in now. Make me focused even though I do not understand where you are taking me. I trust you and yield to your plan. I will not be moved or distracted by this amateur attack.

In Jesus' name, I pray. Amen.

Send Help

Then the Lord God said, "It is not good for the man to be
alone. I will make a helper who is just right for him."
Genesis 2:18 (NLT)

Lately, I have been biting off way more than I can chew. I
have been managing it well, but I am coming to you for help.
Jesus, send the right support, the kind of help that will work
when I do not. Send people that will produce results towards
the vision you have given me. Send the kind of support that
will advocate and be with me forever as you promised in
John 14:16. Whoever you send, allow us to work in unity with
one another.

You can do it, God! You can find anyone on this earth. By
faith, I call forth help. I command trust and obedience to take
over in my life so that I do not miss the help you are sending
my way.

God, I praise you for the help. I pray that you will bless them
for being a blessing to me. Today, I give my load over to you.
I give feeling overwhelmed over to you. I give perfectionism
and procrastination over to you!

I glorify you for making me a leader who knows the value of
collaboration and help. I submit my business plans and goals
to you for final review. I pray that you keep me aligned with
your will and plan.

In Jesus' name, I pray. Amen.

Give God Credit

We can make our plans, but the Lord determines our steps.
Proverbs 16:9 (NLT)

God, to be honest sometimes I do not even know what you see in me. I cannot comprehend or explain how far I have come to get to where I am now. Your love for me is indescribable. I cannot take the credit for anything I have accomplished because without you I would have failed.

I know what it is like to try life without you and I vow never to try again. You proved yourself worthy even before I was born. You are God, the only living God. You provide me with opportunities. You have equipped me with knowledge and wisdom far beyond my background. You have kept me safe. You have allowed me to wake up every day. You constantly extend favor, grace, and mercy to me every day.

You are marvelous and so deserving of my praise and honor. I pray that you would unveil the hidden potential in me that I do not see. Help me to see me through your eyes, God. I owe all to you and just wanted to take the time to acknowledge you today! Continue to have your way in my life.

In Jesus' name, I pray. Amen.

Maximized

Great is our Lord, and of great power: his understanding is infinite.
Psalm 147:5 (KJV)

God, you are big, mighty, and super strong! I know that you are the only one who can do the impossible. You are the most consistent person in my life, and I value our relationship. You are the only one who can fully understand all that I go through.

God, I need your place in my life to be maximized. I desire to be in your will at all times. I will not allow religion to complicate our relationship for you are not a God of confusion.

As I read your word give me clear understanding. Help me to comprehend why you created me. God, I believe that as you are maximized in my life, my life will also be optimized. I decree and declare that my goals, dreams, finances, time, and health will all become maximized.

In Jesus' name, I pray. Amen.

Confidence in You

I remain confident of this: I will see the goodness of the
Lord in the land of the living.
Psalm 27:13 (NIV)

God, I have confidence that you will bless me immediately today. I praise you for a blessing right now. Blessings that are locked up because I was not prepared, release them today.

I declare and decree that I am now prepared. I am in the right mindset to manage my finances. I am ready to fulfill all my responsibilities. I am now walking in the goodness of God! My dream team is coming together right now. I declare that the business plan, resources, the inventions, and investors are coming forth right now in Jesus' name. No more delay or procrastination.

God, I have confidence in you! I believe that I will live to see your goodness shown through my story in this season. God keep preparing me for what is next to come. Keep taking me through everything you destined me to overcome! I have complete confidence in you! I believe that everything you say will come true. I believe it, and I receive it now!

In Jesus' name, I pray. Amen.

Expect and See

For surely there is an end; and thine expectation shall not
be cut off.
Proverbs 23:18 (KJV)

Today, I will put my trust in your hands and wait in
expectation. God, I know you are going to keep your
promises. As long as I do my part, I know you will do yours.
I believe that your role is complete and as I have faith, you
will soon reveal your glory in my life.

Today I am not going to allow space for stress, worry, anger,
or any draining emotions. I claim peace today in Jesus' name.
I will experience joy, and I will be happy today. God set my
day up to be the best day I have ever had. Switch the
trajectory of my days to be more positive and promising.

I decree that I will wake up every day expecting your
goodness to takeover. I pray that I will wake up every day
looking for ways to work my faith. I will be a bold believer
every single day. I will not waiver when things seem slow. I
will not quit when I hear the word no. I will live every day
from here on out in expectation for you to move on my
behalf.

In Jesus' name I pray, Amen!

Time Wasted

Unless the Lord builds the house, the builders labor in vain. Unless the Lord watches over the city, the guards stand watch in vain.
Psalm 127:1 (NIV)

God move me out of your way! I do not want to do anything without you in the midst. I thank you for giving me free will, but I am asking that you show me where I am overstepping my boundaries. If I am putting too much time into man's vision – make it blurry!

Help me to hear you, to see you, and to feel you as I go forth in business, school, work, and relationships. Lay the proper foundation - a steady one so that if I step on any ground that is not of you, I will know.

God, I submit to your instructions so that I am not wasting my time and the time of others. I yield to your plan. Take away anything that you have not destined for me. Give me the courage to remove time-wasting activities and minimize their impact on my progression.

I will stop wasting time, and I will purposefully use the time you have given me. Forgive me for complaining about more time, when I wasted it on many occasions. I decree that time lost is a thing of the past. I will use my time wisely and efficiently. I declare that time will not be a limitation to my success.

In Jesus' name, I pray. Amen.

I Am Great

For we are God's handiwork, created in Christ Jesus to do good works, which God prepared in advance for us to do.
Ephesians 2:10 (NIV)

The enemy wants me to believe that I am confused as to who I am. I was created to do good which means it is good is on the inside of me. No matter what anyone says, I know that I am a good person because Jesus you said so. No, I have not always done good, but I refuse to allow my past to plan my future.

God, I am great because I serve a great God. There has been many circumstances in life that I did not face with faith. Today, I will handle all situations with faith. I will act like I already have the victory because I do. I will perform in greatness. I will love greatly! I will have an attitude, work ethic, and mindset of greatness!

I can be great because there is no reason why I should not be! I decree and declare that I am great because greater is he that is within me, than he that is in the world as it says in 1 John 4:4. Today, I will walk confidently in my greatness.

In Jesus' name, I pray. Amen.

Basic Bites

Do not let your hearts be troubled. You believe in God;
believe also in me.
John 14:1 (NIV)

Today I will believe in you God because you believe in me! I will stop trying to find fault in you because there is none. I will keep my mind focused on you. I have limited myself from believing for your best. Deliver me from being a basic believer and a basic thinker. If I believe basic, I will receive basic.

The moment I begin to doubt is the moment I start to limit the resources available to me. Help me to change my attitude towards life situations. Help me to improve my response to them. I declare that my faith will show in my attitude. When I am sick, struggling, and defeated, I will not have a basic reaction.

Functioning on the basic level will not get me to where I want to be. Cure my basic believing condition! Basic reflects a starting spot and I declare that I will not be in this same position next year.

In Jesus' name, I pray. Amen.

He Did It Again

Jesus Christ the same yesterday, and to day, and for ever.
Hebrews 13:8 (KJV)

God, thank you for never switching up on me. Even in times when you had to discipline me, you did so in love. Regardless of all the hell, I have been through this year I know I am on the other side because of you. Thank you for baring all of my burdens.

You promised never to leave me, and you did not. You are the undefeated champion of the world. You are amazingly refreshing and consistent. No matter what happens in life, I will stand on your never changing word. Who you said you are is who you are.

No longer will I go through life burdened down. I will endure the weight because I know that you will soon lift it. Thank you for doing the heavy lifting God. Thank you for being honest and real with me. Thank you for putting my well-being at the forefront of your mind. God, you made my prayers a priority and answered what was in my best interest. Thank you!

In Jesus' name I pray, Amen!

Guarded

Be always on the watch, and pray that you may be able to escape all that is about to happen, and that you may be able to stand before the Son of Man.
Luke 21:36 (NIV)

Cleanse my mind of all the filth from this year! Any teachings or advice that I have adopted through the year that was deceitful erase it now God. All the lies and traumatic truths from the news, do not let it affect my life to the point of fear and stagnation. God, guard my salvation and protect my peace.

I am your vessel and your temple where you can find rest. I will not allow things to trash your space. Give me the strength to turn off the television, put down my phone, and say no to the things that cause you to be uncomfortable. Forgive me for being careless with your comfort.

Strengthen my senses to perform as a filter of fear and destructive things. Help me to intake more positive and healthy things into my life.

Jesus, I welcome you in to stay and have your way. I confess my sins, and I pray that you will forgive me. Purify me from all unrighteousness as it says in 1 John 1:9.

In Jesus' name, I pray. Amen.

I Have the Power

*Having a form of godliness but denying its power. Have
nothing to do with such people.*
2 Timothy 3:5 (NIV)

God forgive me for denying your power! Forgive me for only
believing when it was easy to believe. Forgive me for
appearing godly but not living in submission to your power.

God, I confess my calling as your child, as your servant, and
vessel. I declare that my life will measure up to the true
believer. I am a follower who believes in you! I will not waste
the power you have given to me.

I call forth power in Jesus' name. I thank you for giving me
the ability to direct my life in a new direction. I have the right
and authority to cast out devils in my life. I have the power to
rebuke the spirit of fear that has held me up. I am free to rule
with the power given from you God.

I will pray always! I declare that my prayers will produce
power! I thank you, God, for the wisdom and power you
have extended to me.

In Jesus' name I pray, Amen!

Stop Grinding

And whatever you do, whether in word or deed, do it all in the name of the Lord Jesus, giving thanks to God the Father through him.
Colossians 3:17 (NIV)

Rest king, rule Lord, and reveal your glory God in my life! Reveal your glory, not my agenda! I have been grinding to become what I view as successful, working tediously and tirelessly to "make it happen."

If "it" is out of your will, redirect my focus. Help me to see my situations through your will. Forgive me if I am running the wrong race. Redirect my steps to be in line with your plan for my life.

Today, I declare that my efforts will not go wasted. My hard work is fulfilling your mission. My grinding days are over. I will not work in a state of oppression, working towards something without an end. God, you promised me an expected end which is in heaven.

I declare that my work will not be in vain. What good is a grind if it keeps me from your promises? In my grinding, I have neglected to rest, which is a necessity. God, you found the value in rest, and I pray you help me to obtain it. Today, I give up trying to out work you.

In Jesus' name, I pray. Amen.

No Prayer, No Power | Amber R. Morson

It Takes Time

*And let us not be weary in well doing: for in due season we
shall reap, if we faint not.*
Galatians 6:9 (KJV)

God, it is frustrating to know that I have sowed freely
without seeing a harvest. I know that I must be patient like
the farmer who works all year to manage the field in
expectation of a harvest. I will not give up! I will not get
bored with sowing good seeds because my harvest is on its
way.

I have sowed good seeds in every aspect, not only tithes and
offering but time, effort, and consistency. You have given me
the option to pick the seeds I plant, and I know that you will
honor them good or bad.

Forgive me for the corrupt seeds I have sowed. Help me to
plant more love, kindness, forgiveness, trust, and loyalty so
that it can return to me. I cannot be upset at the results of my
harvest because all the seeds planted were my choice to sow.

However, I can keep sowing and keep trusting for my good
harvest to come. I decree that better days are coming and I
will not rush the process. I will not let the enemy cause me to
measure my life up to the harvest of seeds others have sown.

I declare that I will honor and praise you along the way for
what you are doing in my life. I will not be a hater but a
praiser because I know that what you do for others you can
do for me. I declare that there will always be a profit in what I
plant.

In Jesus' name, I pray. Amen.

Don't Blame God

But I did find this: God created people to be virtuous, but they have each turned to follow their own downward path."
Ecclesiastes 7:29 (NLT)

God, thank you for free will. I love that you do not force me to make any decisions, but you give me a choice.

You have put before me a road map with clear instructions and repercussions. When I decide to disobey, I delay or alter the route to get to my expected end. Thank you for making the expected end a promise and not a hope. I am praying for the patience to wait in the midst of the restructuring I have caused.

God, I want growth. I want the courage to make the right decisions even if they are the toughest. With growth comes rain. Help me to endure the rain that I essentially asked for. I praise you during the raining because I know it is not going to last forever, it never has.

Forgive me for staying stagnant in the rain because I was too afraid to get wet. Forgive me for not adjusting to the weather because I was too lazy to go back and change things about myself.

Today, I am changing. I am getting ready to face the rain. Whenever I am comfortable I notice it tends to rain longer. Today, I am going to face my discomfort and watch as the rain slows and yields to my faith.

In Jesus' name, I pray. Amen.

Mind Your Business

Don't eavesdrop on others — you may hear your servant
curse you. For you know how often you yourself have
cursed others.
Ecclesiastes 7: 21-22 (NLT)

I must confess that sometimes I am nosey and a gossiper.
God, I try to mind my own business, but sometimes I fail. I
am completely out of your will when I place myself in other
people's business without your permission.

Today, I commit to minding my own business. Experience
tells me that when I go searching for something I am going to
find it. Most times things I discovered hurt me and others in
the process. Help me to be okay with just not knowing or
having the answer.

Forgive me for the times when I was trying to find the flaws
in others. Forgive me for trying to get all the information so I
can take the credit for solving the issue. God, take away all
the satisfaction I feel when I gossip and mind other people's
business. Today, I will focus on you, God.

In Jesus' name, I pray. Amen.

I Mastered It

But thanks be to God, which giveth us the victory through our Lord Jesus Christ.
1 Corinthians 15:57 (KJV)

God, I have done too much to give up now. I have come through too many doors to turn back now. I have defeated the odds set up against me, and I will not throw in the towel.

I have seen you perform too many miracles to doubt you. I have been a recipient of your favor numerous of times to ever think twice about the credibility of your power. I have prayed too many prayers to let go now. God, I have followed you on this jagged journey, and I have no choice but to ride it out.

God, quitting on you profits me nothing. Everything that I have endured was necessary. Help me to see troubles as a prerequisite to victory. I decree and declare that I am a master at overcoming adversity. With you God, I can do all things. By trusting you, I can master any attack that dares to come against me.

Help me to master keeping you at the center of all I do. Help me to master trusting and yielding to you. I pray that when you tell me to give my time and money, I master the art of doing so cheerfully! Thank you for giving me the victory over my circumstances.

In Jesus' name, I pray. Amen.

I've Been Drafted

It is better to trust in the Lord than to put confidence in man.
Psalms 118:8 (KJV)

God, you have set me up to succeed, and you have planted me in a position to prosper. People may think that I am here because of what they have done for me, but you ordained this moment! I thank you for this opportunity. You are the best promise keeper, and I trust you. I am confident in the decision you have made to bring me to this place.

I cannot thank you enough for your faithfulness. I cannot praise you enough for your patience with me. I thank you that every no, and every loss that I endured had a purpose. The purpose helped me to see your strength shine through me. They helped me to realize that I am more than a conqueror through Christ as it says in Romans 8:37.

I will not be fearful going into this new position and season. I do not need to find a clique for loyalty and safety. I will find my refuge in you, Jesus. I know that you appointed me for this opportunity and I am enough to fulfill it.

In Jesus' name, I pray. Amen.

God, You Do It

He must increase, but I must decrease.
John 3:30 (KJV)

I need to stop worrying about things that do not concern me. Yes, I love people and care about them, but at some point, I must let go. It is no justice in helping people if helping is hurting me. I know that you will not step into a situation if you are not petitioned for or welcomed.

God completely letting go of this situation is difficult for me. I am not even sure of how to completely turn it over to you. I want you to know that my spirit is willing to invite you in. My spirit longs for your help because I am not equipped to fix this situation by myself. God, I invite you to come into my life and have your way.

I rebuke my human nature that yearns for me to stay involved. I denounce my fleshly desire to attempt to handle this situation on my own. I cannot change this God only you can. I have tried to pray for what I think is best but I ultimately do not know. All I know is that I am tired of this revolving door.

God, I know you care, and I ask that you increase as I decrease. I pray you see my petition today as genuine and sincere. I have faith that you will turn this mess into a masterpiece.

In Jesus' name, I pray. Amen.

No Locked Doors

And Jesus came and spake unto them, saying, All power is given unto me in heaven and in earth.
Matthew 28:18 (KJV)

They do not know that I am coming but God you know. You planted this arrival, and it is not delayed. God, you are mighty, and the only doors that are closed to me are the ones you have locked. Man will not keep me from what you have in store for me. No one holds more power than you! No one can tell me no after you have already said yes!

God, you rule over everything. You are alpha and omega! Therefore, nothing in my life shall come to an end unless you allow it. I praise and glorify you for keeping your word. Your word said in Matthew 6:4 that when I pray in secret, you will reward openly. God, I thank you for my reward. I see the results of my prayers that I pleaded for you to answer. I thank you for your unlimited grace, favor, and power you reveal to me daily.

In Jesus' name, I pray. Amen.

Take A Step

In all labour there is profit: but the talk of the lips tendeth only to penury.
Proverbs 14:23 (KJV)

If I talk about it, I need to be about it. Today, I am praying for a laboring spirit. I speak about my ideas, goals, and aspirations for hours. God, the same time I spend talking about my goals, help me to do more to push myself closer to achieving them.

God help me not to become complacent in being a dreamer only, help me to put action behind my dreams. Help me to keep taking a step in the right direction daily. Help me to keep moving forward even if I do not see the fruits of my labor yet. Help me to have a persistent prayer life, worshiping, and praising in advance for what is to come.

God, you said that in all labor there would be profit. This means if I keep drafting up contracts, promoting my work, interning, giving 100% at work, attending seminars, and networking, something is going to come out of it. I thank you for the promise in Proverbs 14:23! I thank you that after I say Amen, a laboring spirit will come upon me and poverty will be a thing of the past.

In Jesus' name, I pray. Amen.

Foundation and Focus

If the foundations be destroyed, what can the righteous do?
Psalm 11:3 (KJV)

God, I need you to be the foundation of everything I do. There are some areas in my life where the foundation is not you. Here I am fasting and praying, looking for you to perform when you are not pleased in the first place. Forgive me for wasting my time trying to force you to make what I want your will.

Expose all the areas in my life where you are not the foundation. I thank you that although I have wasted time I have not lost time. I still have time to build towards things with you as the foundation. I still have time to focus on establishing a new career, new relationships, and a healthier lifestyle. I rebuke any negative thought that tries to convince me that time is my limitation. Time will not be a limitation to me because I am walking in alignment with you!

In Jesus' name, I pray. Amen.

Criticism Counts

Better to be criticized by a wise person than to be praised by a fool.
Ecclesiastes 7:5 (NLT)

Sometimes it is hard to see the good in criticism when it comes from the people who are closest to me. It is easy for the enemy to make me place them in the "hater box." Meanwhile, I feel supported when strangers and associates critique me.

Lord, I know that you placed people in my life on assignment. The assignment may be to point me in the right direction to further my goals. It could be for me to see who is purposed to be on this journey with me and who is not. Help me to decipher between the two. Allow the criticism of the wise to resonate in my spirit. For I know Proverbs 15:22 is true when it says that plans fail without counsel and succeed with advisers.

God forgive me for treating the wise in my life as fools. If I insulted anyone's intelligence in the process of them trying to help me - I repent. God, I thank you for the wise and the unwise that offer their input. Bless them for being a motivator and encourager at times. Continue to surround me with wise people. If I am ever criticizing someone, I ask that you allow me to do so in wisdom.

In Jesus' name, I pray. Amen.

Honor God

For I fully expect and hope that I will never be ashamed,
but that I will continue to be bold for Christ, as I have
been in the past. And I trust that my life will bring honor
to Christ, whether I live or die.
Philippians 1:20 (NLT)

Jesus, everything that I do and hope to become I pray that it brings honor to your name. I want to live knowing that through all things you see me as faithful. You can count on me to acknowledge you boldly. I am who I am because you chose to be who your father showed you, you were. Help me to live out the same courage, love, and trust that it took for you to yield to God's will.

Even during the trials I face, help me to have a heart of honor towards you. As people see me, I want them to see the reverence I have for you first. Dead or alive I want to leave a mark as a person who loved, honored, and adored you. Create in me a clean heart and continue to make me more like you so as I stand before you, you are pleased.

In Jesus' name, I pray. Amen.

Learned Behavior

O Lord, you have examined my heart and know everything about me.
Psalm 139:1 (NLT)

God, I want to get to know you better because I do not know you as I should. I desire to have a better relationship with you, and I need your help on how to make this happen. I know that the best way to get to know someone is through spending time and talking with them. I am coming to you right now because I need to talk. I want you to speak with me. God, tune my ears to your voice.

I have heard many stories about you and have made my judgments based off stories. I learned about you as a child, but I am older now and desire to know you for myself. I am in a place where I long to have a personal connection with you. I want to know you as you know me.

Remove the nervousness, suspicion, shame, and any guilt that I feel when I come before you. For your word instructs me to come boldly before you in Hebrews 4:16. Teach me how to communicate with you. Allow me to experience the benefits of the believer who spends time with you. Show me how to minimize the influence of the naysayers who do not approve of our relationship. I rebuke anything that tries to get in the way of me learning you for myself.

In Jesus' name, I pray. Amen.

Exposed

Not a single person on earth is always good and never sins.
Ecclesiastes 7:20 (NLT)

I will not live in shame anymore. I will not stay silent in secrecy out of fear of being judged. God, I need you! Devil, you are a liar, and you will not keep me bound anymore.

God, I am a sinner who is only saved because of your grace. Your word says this, so I know that sinning is not something that you thought I would not do. You knew that I would encounter sin at some point in my life. I know that you have given me the tools to overcome sin. I also know that I can always come to you for forgiveness when I mess up.

I confess that I have done wrong and I ask that you forgive me. Today, I expose Satan and the sins I have committed. I thank you for the team of prayer warriors you assigned for me at this very moment. I decree freedom right now. I call forth fresh oil and a new anointing. I declare that I am free from sin and every shackle is broken in my life!

In Jesus' name, I pray. Amen.

No Excuses

But be ye doers of the word, and not hearers only,
deceiving your own selves.
James 1:22 (KJV)

Excuses are tools of incompetence that will lead me to a place
I do not desire to be. God, I have heard of you every since I
was a child. Now as an adult I still hear about you. God, I
know what you expect out of me, help me to act accordingly.
Not only have I heard, but I can read and apply your
principles to my life.

God rid me of all my pride and foolishness that prevents me
from doing what your word instructs. I pray that you give me
a revelation of your word to help me understand things I
question. Bring clarity to me when I hear your word so that I
can be quick to apply it to my life.

I do not want to jeopardize my relationship with you because
I pick and choose when and what to believe. I believe that all
your word is true!

James 2:10 warns me that I will be accountable for the laws I
do not follow. Help me to take heed to your instructions and
do as they all say.

In Jesus' name, I pray. Amen.

The Return

Let the redeemed of the Lord say so, who he hath redeemed
from the hand of the enemy.
Psalm 107:2 (KJV)

God, you are my redeemer and present help. You are all that
I could ever need in this life. You are marvelous and
forgiving! I thank you for showering me with your
redeeming love. Even if my actions were intentionally poor
your grace and your mercy never ran dry!

Thank you for seeing me as redemption worthy. Thank you
for looking past my wrong and seeing that I still had good in
me. Thank you for making a return on the little that I
invested.

I take responsibility for all of my faults, and you still see fit to
restore me. You have completely freed me! You have refined
every one of my flaws and downfalls.

I will tell of your goodness and grace forever.

In Jesus' name, I pray. Amen.

Commanded Not Suggested

Then Moses called together the whole community of Israel and told them, "These are the instructions the Lord has commanded you to follow.
Exodus 35:1 (NLT)

I pray that as I read your word, I come to know your commandments. I pray that I become the things you ordained me to be. I confess Psalm 119:105 over my life which says that your word is a lamp unto my feet. God, provide the light for my path.

You commanded me "to be" over 50 times throughout scripture. You did not say to become you said, "to be" which means to occur now. I declare that I will be all that you have called me to be. I am thankful, patient, and courageous. I am sober, vigilant, and a doer of your word. I decree that I am careful to maintain good works and I am content with the blessings you have given me.

I will apply your commandments to my life. I will do the things you asked of me because I know they are all in my best interest. I will no longer view your commandments as suggestions. I will treat your commandments as such and not lean unto my own understanding.

In Jesus' name, I pray. Amen.

Enjoy Life

There is nothing better for a man, than that he should eat and drink, and that he should make his soul enjoy good in his labour. This also I saw, that it was from the hand of God.
Ecclesiastes 2:24 (KJV)

God, you came so that I could live an abundant life. You want me to be prosperous and happy. Your word says in 1 Timothy 6:17, that you give us all things to enjoy. I believe this, and I accept it for what it is. I will not allow people to make me feel bad for liking specific brands, going on certain trips, and spending my money on what I want.

I decree that this is my year to experience eternal joy! The best happiness that life can offer, I receive it now! I decree that blessings are coming to me right now. Windows of opportunities are being opened for me to have the means to live in abundance.

I call forth abundant living right now because God you commanded it. I will be confident and not ashamed of the blessings you have bestowed upon me. I will laugh, have fun, and enjoy this life the way that you intended!

In Jesus' name, I pray. Amen.

Finish It

*Be ye strong therefore, and let not your hands be weak: for
your work shall be rewarded.*
2 Chronicles 15:7 (KJV)

God grant me the grace to finish what I start. Position me into
the right place to focus on finishing! The same courage I had
to start, revive it in me so that I can finish. Keep my mind
stayed on the purpose of my start. Give me a glimpse into the
blessing that will manifest once the mission, goal, or tasks are
complete.

I rebuke the spirit of procrastination and laziness. I rebuke
the urge to compare my work to others. I cancel out the
thoughts that tell me I must run my plans by people before
moving forward.

The devil is a liar, and he is a joke! He will not steal, kill, and
destroy me in the middle. I will fight through the middle
until I make it to the end. God, you did not say the work
would be easy, but you did say there will be a reward if I do
not give up.

In Jesus' name, I pray. Amen.

And the Winner Is

For the flesh lusteth against the Spirit, and the Spirit against the flesh: and these are contrary the one to the other: so that ye cannot do the things that ye would.
Galatians 5:17 (KJV)

Spirit in the name of Jesus I pronounce you the winner! You have defeated flesh. Spirit you will remain strong and come to know what you are capable of through Christ Jesus. Anything that tries to war against you will be cast down.

Spirit, I command you to rise and build towers of truth around me daily. Block out the noise that tries to draw me nearer to sin and further from my faith. Spirit you will not struggle to stay sane.

God, you are Jehovah Nissi, my victory! Jehovah Shammah, my very present help. Jehovah Raah, the remover of all my fears. You are my God the winner in every battle, the answer to every test! I declare my flesh the weakest link. I will do what I know I am supposed to because my spirit will win.

In Jesus' name, I pray. Amen.

Stress Reliever

In the multitude of my thoughts within me thy comforts delight my soul.
Psalm 94:19 (KJV)

God, I am stressed, but I know you to be Jehovah Shalom my peace. Cause my stress to flee before the seconds' change. You are the subject of my faith, and my trust is in you.

Jesus, your name holds all working power! Jesus, work your power to silence the things that are working my nerves. I declare that today will be a stress-free day.

I decree that my soul will be comforted today. At this moment, I am beginning to feel weights lift. My mind is at ease, and my body is relaxed. I am thinking about your goodness, and it is sustaining me.

Thank you, Jesus, for releasing me today. Thank you for being a stress reliever at this moment. Thank you for your Philippians 4:7 peace, that has surpassed my understanding.

In Jesus' name, I pray. Amen.

Old School Faith

Let perseverance finish its work so that you may be
mature and complete, not lacking anything.
James 1:4 (NIV)

Today, I will experience the joy in my purpose and not the pain. I will focus my attention on the gain that is coming from the pain I am enduring. I declare that my faith will not waver. God your word is clearing the darkness from my path. It is giving me hope as I wait on you.

I believe that things are not what they seem. Things are not as far away as I may think. I trust that you will answer my prayers. I have no other choice but to trust you and stand on your word. I will wait patiently on you Lord – for your timing has no faults. Forgive me for questioning you. I know that you are not moved by my lack of understanding only my faith.

I pray that you help me fine tune my faith until it becomes consistent. I will persevere in all things and will lack nothing.

In Jesus' name, I pray. Amen.

Speak the Word

For the word of God is alive and active. Sharper than any double-edged sword, it penetrates even to dividing soul and spirit, joints and marrow; it judges the thoughts and attitudes of the heart.
Hebrews 4:12 (NIV)

God, I believe that I can have whatever I say! I know that I will have whatever you promised. I will stand on the promises you have made to me through scripture. Today, I will speak the word.

In Philippians 4:19 you said that all of my needs you will supply. Therefore, I command every financial problem to flee from my life. I confess that I am in good health for you endured stripes to free me from sickness and heal me from diseases according to Isaiah 53:5.

I will not let evil and negative people get the best of me because blessings are attached to the evilness they bestow according to 1 Peter 3:9. I declare that I am not afraid because God you promised me protection and comfort in Psalm 23.

God, thank you for the word. I know that nothing the devil throws at me is enough to strike me out. In John 16:33 it says that you have overcome the world, this means nothing can defeat me if I follow you.

God, forgive me for speaking more about my issues than I do your word. Today I will stop referencing the problems and reference the promises.

In Jesus' name, I pray. Amen.

No Prayer, No Power | Amber R. Morson

Decisions, Decisions, Decisions

I will instruct thee and teach thee in the way which thou shalt go: I will guide thee with mine eye.
Psalm 32:8 (KJV)

I declare that I am a good decision maker. I know I made some bad decisions in my past, but the good will outweigh the bad this year. Now, I am wiser, better, and I carefully apply the word of God to my life. I am free from sin so any decision I make shall bring glory to God.

Decisions that I make are impacting lives for the better. I decree that sound decisions come naturally to me. I am free from toiling over decisions while being torn in my thoughts. My decisions will not keep me from excelling forward.

Today, I will decide my way into a breakthrough. I will decide my way into my purpose. I will decide my way into love, peace, and happiness with your help God. Today, I have decided to change my method of decision making to reflect faith, focus, and results. I decree and declare that my decisions will line up with the word.

In Jesus' name, I pray. Amen.

You Said It

God is not a man, that he should lie; neither the son of man, that he should repent: hath he said, and shall he not do it? or hath he spoken, and shall he not make it good?
Numbers 23:19 (KJV)

God, I am not experiencing some things you promised me as your child. I pray that you do not think I am trying to rush your process. I am only coming before you boldly to remind you of the things that you promised me.

God, you said that if I work diligently and put forth hard work that I would prosper. Bring forth my seasons of prosperity that you granted me in Proverbs 13:4. I pray that within a week good things are going to start multiplying. My faith is going to cause things in the spirit to flourish in the earth.

Show me who to bless as you bless me. Someone will not go without because I have put in the work. Working is not solely for my benefit, but it is to benefit others as it says in Ephesians 4:28.

God, build me up with the strength that is produced through peace and confidence as it says in Isaiah 30:15. God, place peace in my mind, spirit, soul, and body. I thank you for hearing my plea and for releasing the things you said are mine!

In Jesus' name, I pray. Amen.

Unity

How good and pleasant it is when God's people live
together in unity!
Psalm 133:1 (NIV)

Unity is on its way to my house. I command unity to take its rightful place throughout my life. Lord use me to set the standard for love and respect in my home, on my job, and in my relationships. I have had enough with arguing, nagging, yelling, fighting, and feeling in isolation every time I speak.

Unspeakable joy meet me where I am. Every place that I travel and to every person I speak with I command joy and unity to be present. I command unity to linger in all the places that I go so that others can benefit from positive spaces.

God, I pray that you help me to be a unified front standing in submission to you with my family and friends. Help me to get along with others. If I am the problem correct my actions that cause division and mess. Help me to get along with all people, even with the people who do not acknowledge you as God. Humble and mature me so that I can still show love and respect to them.

Today, I expect unity to show up in all the areas that division exists in my life.

In Jesus' name, I pray. Amen.

Joy and Justice

When justice is done, it brings joy to the righteous but terror to evildoers.
Proverbs 21:15 (NIV)

There will be joy in the justice that is coming to me and my family. This time justice is not going to hurt. Not only is the truth going to come out but all parties indirectly involved will be set free. God, set us free from the chains of reactionary violence, poor decision making, and the pain that plagues our hearts and minds.

God, protect and strengthen us to live through the judgment. Right every wrong and renew right spirits in everyone. Change us and make us more like you.

Remove us from out of the reach of our enemies' hands. I am trusting in you to keep us safe from evil people. Protect us, God. Forgive us for any part we played and for turning the other cheek when we could have corrected bad behavior.

In Jesus' name, I pray. Amen.

Stop It Now

To put off your old self, which belongs to your former manner of life and is corrupt through deceitful desires, and to be renewed in the spirit of your minds, and to put on the new self, created after the likeness of God in true righteousness and holiness.
Ephesians 4:22 – 24 (ESV)

No more trying, planning, hoping, and wishing – it is now or never! Today, I am going to stop engaging in things that are no good for me. I will start to love again and stop being content with numbness. God, help me to get back in tune with my feelings because you gave them to me to help me learn and grow.

I will stop claiming lack. I will labor in expectation of miracles, blessings, and favor. I will work to see your work, working in my life. I will stop all excuses! I will cease laziness and stop entertaining preventers of my purpose.

Today will be the funeral for my old mindset and backward living. Thank you, Lord, for waking me up this morning and giving me a chance to start again. An opportunity to view life through your perfect lenses. Thank you for giving me the power to say no to things that are a deterrent to my relationship with you.

In Jesus' name, I pray. Amen.

I am Innocent

For whosoever will save his life shall lose it: and
whosoever will lose his life for my sake shall find it.
Matthew 16: 25 (KJV)

I did not do what people are saying I did. I did not say what
they are excusing me of saying. If anything, I might have
thought about it, and I ask that you forgive me for that. God
intervene on my behalf and fight for me. I cannot save myself
from this situation. I need your help.

God, I feel left although I know you have not gone. I will not
attempt to come to my rescue because your blood covers me.
What I will do is take up my cross and follow you regardless
of how or if you chose to intervene. I will trust you regardless
of what path you have me on.

I will not turn on you because people have turned on me. I
am good because you are great! I am safe and will be free
from all charges as you see fit. I am right where you need me
to be, for me to get to what you have for me.

In Jesus' name, I pray. Amen.

Leave Now

Ye have not chosen me, but I have chosen you, and ordained you, that ye should go and bring forth fruit, and that your fruit should remain: that whatsoever ye shall ask of the Father in my name, he may give it you.
John 15:16 (KJV)

God, staying stagnant in this place is going to kill me. I cannot afford to keep being here, waiting here, and settling for safe here. Help me to get out of this comfort zone before I smother my growth and potential. Today is the day I must go. Speak to my mind Holy Spirit and speak to my instincts.

Pull me out of this place! Throw me overboard so I can fall amongst the great. Expand the horizons of my mind. Open me up, empty me out, and fill me with the faith to move forward. Give me the confidence to act on your word!

I decree that I am strong enough to leave. I am good enough to make it elsewhere. I will succeed, and I will grow wherever I go. I will be fruitful, and my fruit will remain.

In Jesus' name, I pray. Amen.

Let It Out

You have turned my mourning into joyful dancing. You have taken away my clothes of mourning and clothed me with joy.
Psalm 30:11 (NLT)

Emotions are not a sin. God, I am not convinced that expressing my feelings, which you gave to me are built to make me weak. I will verbalize my emotions this year. I will release all the emotions bottled inside me that I thought were keeping me safe. Bottled emotions are not making me safe they are making me numb and shallow.

God, my feelings were hurt, and it hurts even to attempt to release it. Laughing is not enough to overshadow my disappointments and pain. Your word says in Proverbs 14:12, that laughter can only conceal my heavy heart, but when it ends my grief will remain. I do not want any sadness, anger, or hurt to stay in me. I decree that releasing the pain will not kill me. I claim my freedom today. Evict the emptiness that lingers in my heart. God, bind me with your love wherever I am hurt.

I feel your presence with me at this very moment. Saturate me with your love and care. I sense you moving in me. I am beginning to feel and heal again. Thank you for taking the pain I let out and for replacing it with joy.

In Jesus' name, I pray. Amen.

It's My Turn

Every good and perfect gift is from above, coming down
from the Father of the heavenly lights, who does not
change like shifting shadows.
James 1:17 (NIV)

The moment has arrived for me to be next in line. I decree
that today is blessing time! Thank you for gracing me with
the patience to make it this far. I am grateful that I did not
give up my spot out of weariness. I stayed in this with you,
and you sustained me. There is nobody anywhere like you
Jesus.

You do not do the bare minimum so I know I am in for a
breathtaking treat. No words are going to be able to describe
the blessings in store for me in this season. God, I thank you
now. I praise, worship, and magnify you. You are a good,
good, good father! You did not leave out, and I appreciate
you! You make all things new. You make all blessings bigger
than the ones before.

Things get better when I spend my time with you! You show
out when I show up! God, I praise you in advance for what
you are getting ready to do. Thank You, God.

In Jesus' name I pray, Amen!

Bounce Back

For though the righteous fall seven times, they rise again,
but the wicked stumble when calamity strikes.
Proverbs 24: 16 (NIV)

The devil thinks he has me, but I will remind him of who I am. I am a bounce back believer! If I go down, I will come back up. Today, the ball is back in my court, and I am ending the game. I have overcome sin, hurt, harm, and danger because greater is on the inside of me. I am a child of King Jesus, and no one can knock me off my throne of grace.

I declare that my ability to bounce back from tough situations will be easier this year. I survived what could have broken me last year, and I thank you God for giving me the strength.

I am back, and I am already better. I am stronger than I was when I fell. I am a top-shelf believer. I cannot be touched by Satan because he is beneath me. God, thank you for your angels who encompass around me daily.

In Jesus' name, I pray. Amen.

Future Focused

Yet what we suffer now is nothing compared to the glory he will reveal to us later.
Romans 8:18 (NLT)

My future is not fake. It is not a fantasy of what is to come. God, I believe that my future is a destination destined by you. I will remain excited about what is to come.

Faith and focus will be my motto for today. I will get things done. I will reach my short-term goals for they will lead me to accomplish my long-term ones. I will increase my effort and effectiveness today.

I will not minimize my goals because the work is hard! I will not take the easy way out. I will go down the road less traveled, and I will get reach the expected end. Folding under pressure is not an option. I declare that because I was birthed from pressure my future will be too. I declare that the pressure will not stop me. It will only make me better.

In Jesus' name, I pray. Amen.

Money Talks

The blessing of the Lord makes a person rich, and he adds no sorrow with it.
Proverbs 10:22 (NLT)

Money talks but so does the Holy Spirit! I declare that today, money that is not in my possession is being spent to help me. I declare blessing from the hands of people who I do not know. People are beginning to pour into my purpose. People who I may never know are believing in my product, buying my goods, and services.

I decree that lack has no space in my life. Miracles are happening out of nowhere. Things are changing daily, and my name is circling in high places. Thank you, Lord, for the people who put my name in the atmosphere. Thank you for keeping me in the hearts and minds of millions of people.

I do not deserve your unmerited favor. God, let these words of my mouth and the meditation of my heart be acceptable in your sight. For you are my strength, my redeemer, and all these things are possible with you.

In Jesus' name, I pray. Amen.

Get in Order

Let all things be done decently and in order.
1 Corinthians 14:40 (KJV)

God, you have done too many marvelous things for me to still live out of order. I cannot keep praying for more blessings if I am struggling to manage what I have now. My prayer today is that you help me to get in order.

I pray away the desire to be impressed with basic effort and weak gestures. It is not enough just to get a calendar, exercise, diet, and wake up at the crack of dawn. They are all decent things to try, but it is not creating order if you are not my first priority. I pray that you help me to find and keep order.

Today, I will seek you first as you have instructed me to do in Matthew 6:33. Spending time with you is the best start for my day. Only after I seek, you will I be able to have a good day. I pray for more patience in my spirit. Strengthen my spirit to delay the things that have been my normal go-to routine in the morning, so that you can be first.

In Jesus' name, I pray. Amen.

It's Paid

The wicked borroweth, and payeth not again: but the
righteous sheweth mercy, and giveth.
Psalm 37:21 (KJV)

God, I declare that my bills are paid in full. Balances are no longer bothering me because this is my season to be debt free. Lenders are beginning to lower and eliminate interest rates at this very moment. Banks and debt collectors are calling to tell me good news. By faith, I believe that my debts are forgiven. By faith, I declare that all my bills will be paid in full for the rest of my life!

My credit is beginning to recover because God you are the restorer of all things. Places that did not approve me are calling to say, "there must have been a mistake." I pray for approval in the name of Jesus. My bills are going down this year. My mortgage is decreasing. My car note is lowering. My insurance is being cut in half! Rebates are being released in my name. Medical bills are being paid in full, and tuition is being covered by grants and scholarships – right now!

Increase as I decrease God! Make me the lender and not the borrower. Place me in a position where I can freely give, expecting nothing in return.

In Jesus' name, I pray. Amen.

Love Like God

Love must be sincere. Hate what is evil; cling to what is good.
Romans 12:9 (NIV)

God forgive me for showing love on stipulations and conditions. I pray that my love will be a free gift to others because you gave me yours at no cost. Show me how to love the lost and those who do not even like themselves.

I do not know where I would be if you decided to only love me based on how I treated myself. If you made me earn your love, I would not have it today. I will begin to love more as you love. I will not regret loving anyone because love is not about me it is a reflection of you.

People can no longer steal my right to love or punish me for it. I refuse to believe that taking my love away is a better option. If I do not love, then I hate, and I will not live in hatred anymore.

Disappointments that come with loving others freely will not break me. I declare that I will not be deceived or used. I am smart and God you are on my side. Teach me to guard my heart above all things as you have instructed in Proverbs 4:23! In Jesus' name, I pray. Amen.

Run the Race

I have seen something else under the sun: The race is not to the swift or the battle to the strong, nor does food come to the wise or wealth to the brilliant or favor to the learned; but time and chance happen to them all.
Ecclesiastes 9:11 (NIV)

My parents lived their own lives and had their successes and struggles. I pray for the same courage they showed by allowing me to come into the world. Whether they were the best parents or the worst, I am here because of them.

I forgive my parents for the scars they gave to me intentionally and unintentionally. I love them for all they could be and do for me. Now, something in me wants more. I am trusting that I have more and can do more than what they did.

God, give me the dedication to run with the baton that my parents passed on to me. I decree a finished race in Jesus' name. I declare that the beginning of a new legacy is at the finish line. God, allow newness to begin with me. New favor, fresh oil, infinite wealth, and opportunities are coming and staying in my bloodline.

Wealth will not ruin my family for we will stay grounded in the principles of your word. I decree that time, and chance will work in my favor in this lifetime!

In Jesus' name, I pray. Amen.

Fakes & Haters

Remember what I told you: 'A servant is not greater than his master.' If they persecuted me, they will persecute you also. If they obeyed my teaching, they will obey yours also.
John 15:20 (NIV)

Lord Jesus, I am struggling to fight off certain things. Haters are not going anywhere, and fake people are not either. Someone is always going to have something to say, help me to be okay with this. People talked about you, so I know I am not exempt.

By faith, I am entering a new phase in my life. A phase where I am not hung up on what people have to say about me. I refuse to spend time this year getting to the bottom of situations rooted in false cares and concerns.

Everyone does not like me and that is okay. At this very moment, I decree that I am getting over it. Everyone did not like you Jesus, but you still reign high above all. Since you are victorious through the backstabbing by those who despise you, I can be too.

Fake people will not stop the progress!

In Jesus' name, I pray. Amen.

My Voice

Let your conversation be always full of grace, seasoned with salt, so that you may know how to answer everyone.
Colossians 4:6 (NIV)

God, why did you give me a voice? I often hesitate to use it when it is easier just to stay silent. Sometimes when I do attempt to speak I feel as though no one fully hears me.

I am coming to you because I have lost my voice and I need it back. I believe that you gave me my voice as a blessing. I need to get back in tune with who I am, what I think, and want. Lately, my response to everything has been "I do not care" or "whatever works." No! Whatever does not work, I do care, and I have thoughts to bring to the table.

Whatever happened that caused this silence, I pray that you help me to realize my voice matters. Help me to use it again in a way that glorifies you and brings out the best in others! I thank you for my voice as some people cannot even speak at all.

Today, I am going to speak up and use the voice and mind you gave to me.

In Jesus' name, I pray. Amen.

Set Apart

*And all nations will hate you because you are my
followers. But everyone who endures to the end will be
saved.*
Matthew 10:22 (NLT)

God, I desire to be more confident as I walk in my calling. Be
my strength when not fitting in takes a toll on me.

Going certain places and following certain trends is not what
I was created to do. You did not create me to be a savage, liar,
or hater. God, you have set me apart. I pray that you give me
the sense to follow you when others do not. Forgive me for
trying to fit in when you have called me to stand out.

Thank you for making me something like a limited-edition
car. Thank you for building me to stand out and sustain the
test of time. I am a luxury, bought only at a high price.
Continue to show me the environments that are not suitable
for me to go. My prayer is that you continue to guide me on
where I should go. Remove the desires from me that have led
me down paths too narrow for my makeup.

In Jesus' name, I pray. Amen.

Can't Rush God

The Lord isn't really being slow about his promise, as
some people think. No, he is being patient for your sake.
He does not want anyone to be destroyed, but wants
everyone to repent.
2 Peter 3:9 (KJV)

I decree your timing God, not mines. I will stop being
anxious and pray for a spirit of patience to resonate in my
soul. Time is not of the essence because God your timing is
perfect. You know what I need and when I need it. I declare
that time is not a limitation to my success.

I will not fear time running out or be anxious about the
possibility of missed opportunities. God, you are the supplier
of time. I am confident that every opportunity you bring me
to you will bring me through. Bless me on your account, not
mine. My impatience will not move you any faster, so I pray
that you help me to relax.

I declare today to be a day of patience and long-suffering.
Build up my spiritual stamina to make it through when
things seem to be moving slow. I will wait on you, God. I
repent of all my sins, and I decree that unconfessed sins will
not hold me up from receiving the things you promised.

In Jesus' name, I pray. Amen.

Silence Society

Wherefore take unto you the whole armour of God, that ye may be able to withstand in the evil day, and having done all, to stand.
Ephesians 6:13 (KJV)

Lying, cheating, deceitfulness, backstabbing, and hatred will not be a regular part of my personality or character. They will not be a part of my day. Today will be a good day! I am going back to my God-given roots, and I will place love and loyalty into the atmosphere.

My standards every day will start and end with you Jesus, not with society! Today my mind will be free from corruption. Today my spiritual standards will remain high. I will block out anything that can taint my mind, haunt my hopes, or sabotage my success.

I will not keep jeopardizing my spiritual sanity at the hands of society. I do not have to "stay woke" at the expense of my peace of mind. As I take time to pray today, I will release the things sitting in my mind that are causing my brain to rust. All the residue from reality television, news, and social media will not cause me to lean on my understanding but to rely more heavily on yours.

In Jesus' name, I pray. Amen.

Wonder Woman

She carefully watches everything in her household and
suffers nothing from laziness.
Proverbs 31:27 (NLT)

God, you knew what I needed! I thank you for the strong
selfless woman you handpicked to be in my life. I pray that I
someday embody the same strength, courage, and faith that
she has. She mustered up the faith to look me in my face and
tell me when I was wrong. She did not encourage my faults
instead she prayed against them. Her wisdom and kindness
truly reflect the woman you designed in Proverbs 31.

I thank you for placing an example of a strong woman in my
life. She was never too strong not to lean on you. I pray for
the same strength, belief, and trust in you. Today, I honor you
for honoring her.

In Jesus' name, I pray. Amen.

Say It

Only ask, and I will give you the nations as your inheritance, the whole earth as your possession.
Psalm 2:8 (NLT)

If I can open my mouth to say it, I can train my mind to look for it. This week will be one of anticipation and expectancy! The things that I declare and decree today will come to past this week without delay. As I pray today, God, censor my speech and do not let me ask for anything you do not want me to have. Search my heart and make my intentions pure in Jesus' name.

I decree fresh favor to saturate me this week. I decree a douse of deliverance out from under anything, not like you God. I decree that generational chains will be broken and never locked again. I decree freedom from anything that has me bound. I decree a release from guilt and humiliation. I decree protection, healing, and health.

God, I declare that you will get the glory out of my life. Your goodness will overflow week after week after week. I declare mighty to be the works of your hands this week and every week after!

In Jesus' name, I pray. Amen.

When the Answer Is No

For verily I say unto you, that whosoever shall say unto this mountain, be thou removed, and be thou cast into the sea; and shall not doubt in his heart, but shall believe that those things which he saith shall come to pass; he shall have whatsoever he saith.
Mark 11:23 (KJV)

God, I stood on your word. I have followed what you said, but my mountains have not moved. I have prayed prayers and still no answer. Show me the hills in my life that should be removed by me. Reveal to me what mountains need to be climbed over or even left alone for my safety.

Today, I will be courageous, and strong for I have the power to move mountains. My power to move mountains comes from my ability to say "no."

"No," I am not staying in a bad relationship. "No," I am not going to keep getting high and drunk. "No," I will not keep insulting you with my sin. "No," I am not going back. I am going to stop being an absent parent, stop being a disrespectful child, and a selfish person.

My "no" is moving the mountains! Help me to say what I mean and to mean what I say so the mountains will stop reappearing. Forgive me for creating my mountains and blaming you for not moving them. I declare that I am my own answered prayer. You gave me the power to use in all situations not only against the enemy but to overcome my inner me. I declare no more wasted power this year!

In Jesus' name, I pray. Amen.

No Prayer, No Power | Amber R. Morson

Instant Gratification

Wait on the Lord: be of good courage, and he shall strengthen thine heart: wait, I say, on the Lord.
Psalm 27:14 (KJV)

God, I live in expectation of miracles, blessings, and answered prayers. I am always anticipating your next move because I know you are going to perform. I pray that when you move, I move into a greater understanding of who I am.

Do not bless me until I am ready Lord. I do not want microwaveable blessings - make my blessing from scratch! Take your time, season me with strength, and let it marinate. Cook me with the oils from your anointing. Serve me in due time and due season.

God, remove my desire for instant gratification. I do not want the shortcut or the easy way out. I pray that I am stronger because I fought through the valley. I am wiser because of the wait. Build my faith as I pray for what is right not what is quick and easy. I come against the spirit of instant gratification and pray for the wisdom to wait.

In Jesus' name, I pray. Amen.

Worthless

But even the very hairs of your head are all numbered. Fear not therefore: ye are of more value than many sparrows.
Luke 12:7 (KJV)

My sins will not devalue my life. Thank you, God, for not allowing the things I have done to separate me from your love. No sin, lie, or wrong decision was more powerful than your grace. I will always be worth more to you.

I pray that you help me to see my worth the way that you see it. Help me to find my purpose in the triviality that I sometimes feel. I decree that my purpose is worthwhile because you can still use me. I declare that I hold good qualities that will be used to flourish my future forward.

Feelings of self-doubt, insecurities, and inadequacies will no longer taunt me. God, I feel better, and I look better than I was yesterday. I decree happiness, gratitude, and positivity in my mind. Whenever I look in the mirror, I will see the beauty you exchanged for my ashes.

My worth is not up for debate because no one can place value on me but you Lord. Thank you for paying the ultimate price for me.

In Jesus' name, I pray. Amen.

The Benefits Package

They shall take up serpents; and if they drink any deadly thing, it shall not hurt them; they shall lay hands on the sick, and they shall recover.
Mark 16:18 (KJV)

God, I believe that there is a purpose beyond my paycheck. As a believer, I reap the benefits of being an heir of your blessings. Use my life to translate your offer of salvation to those who have not yet accepted it so they can reap the benefits of a believer too.

I have the authority to take dominion over everything that the word says belongs to me. I can cast out devils, speak privately to you, and tread upon things designed to hurt me and they will not be able to. Through the touch of my hand, the sick can recover. I can sin and still be loved by you. I have your favor that will transfer throughout generations. Mercy and grace will follow me all the days of my life.

With your instructions, I can reach my full potential, and goals. God, help me to maximize my benefits in you. Thank you for believer benefits that come at a low cost graced with a large return.

In Jesus' name, I pray. Amen.

You Hear Me

I love the Lord, because he hath heard my voice and my supplications.
Psalm 116:1 (KJV)

I cry out to you Lord; please hear my plea, and my request for help when no one else is listening. Clear up any feelings of confusion, fear, and frustration that I may have. Even when I do not know what is wrong, you do. Exalt my thoughts with your intentions so that I can rest in the release of your mercy and grace.

God, you are assertive, and you hear my cries when I do not utter a sound. You are there for me when I feel down. I cannot pretend when I am in your presence. Relieve me from any pressure, sadness, and anxiety. Drench me with your peace so that I may have a restful night. Fill the gaps in my heart with your love.

Clothe me with an armor that protects me from compassion fatigue. Embrace me with your forgiving arms. Wrap me tight in your tender care. Guard my mind against the darkness that tries to sneak in while I am asleep. Thank you for hearing my prayers.

In Jesus' name, I pray. Amen.

Bring Them Home

*And this hope will not lead to disappointment. For we
know how dearly God loves us, because he has given us
the Holy Spirit to fill our hearts with his love.*
Romans 5:5 (NLT)

My prayer today is that you watch over your people. So
many people are going missing. Children are running away,
adults are disappearing, and people are being murdered
every day. I pray for protection over your people today God.

I pray for a spiritual fence to govern my mind and the minds
of your people. Silence the voices of depression, madness,
suicide, helplessness, and death that tries to speak to us. Cast
jealously and hatred back into the pits of hell.

Restore peace into our minds and hope into our homes. I
decree the missing to be found safe and sound. Restore the
memory of the lost and allow them to trace back home.

I bind Satan in the name of Jesus! I declare a safe return of all
the people who are missing.

In Jesus' name, I pray. Amen.

Family & Friends

Do everything in love.
1 Corinthians 16:14 (NIV)

God, where you are taking me everyone cannot go. I realize people I thought would always be in my corner are the same ones who pushed me in the current corner that has me stuck. God, reveal the people to me that are not really for me. Help me to get past the pain that will come with losing people I thought were loyal.

God, I will not question your decisions. I will trust you no matter who you expose. I pray that I will have the wisdom to accept the things I cannot change and grow from them. God, do not let me be bitter or angry after the truth is revealed. Help me to do things in love regardless out the outcome.

I pray that every person you remove, you replace.

In Jesus' name, I pray. Amen.

The Thin Line

*Never pay back evil with more evil. Do things in such a
way that everyone can see you are honorable.*
Romans 12:17 (NLT)

God, help me to see the line between helping and being taken
advantage of when it comes to being there for people. Being
used does not feel good. However, when you do not realize
you are being used the feeling of helping is often a pleasant
one.

Today, I pray that you expose all the users. Make the thin line
bold, so I can see when the enemy sends people fake people
into my life. I decree that helping others will not hurt or
hinder me from doing the things you have called me to do.
Expose the people who are only looking for handouts and not
help.

I will no longer be punked into helping people who try to
guilt me into doing things for them. Remove people from my
circle who are only around to benefit from my success. God, I
pray that you touch their hearts and purify their intentions.

God help me to say no when I should not be saying yes. Help
me to see that saying no does not mean I am a selfish person.
Help me to know the difference between an assignment from
you and a self-inflicted obligation that I place on myself.

In Jesus' name, I pray. Amen.

Private Prayers

But when you pray, go into your room, close the door and pray to your Father, who is unseen. Then your Father, who sees what is done in secret, will reward you.
Matthew 6:6 (NIV)

God, forgive me for not asking for help when I knew I needed it. I know you were the one leading me to make my request known and I did not. I allowed fear to get the best of me and I did not speak up.

Today, I pray for guidance. Show me which way I should turn next. The prayers that I pray in private and am too scared to share with others mean just as much to me as those I do share. God, I pray that you meet me in this private place where I am comfortable to be open with you.

God, I lay everything out on the table. I know that you have no respect of persons and you love us all just the same. God, move in my life today. Saturate me with the strength to accept the answers you will provide to my prayers. God, I do not doubt you. I trust that as I pray in private, you will reward opening to receive the glory.

In Jesus' name, I pray. Amen.

Present

You make known to me the path of life; you will fill me with joy in your presence, with eternal pleasures at your right hand.
Psalm 16:11 (NIV)

God, thank you for waking me up today. Thank you for the activity of my limbs and for watching over me yesterday. I thank you for giving me another opportunity to allow your glory to flow through me.

I pray that you help me, to be present in your presence today. Take me off autopilot and allow me to feel, taste, and see how great you are. I do not want to miss the joy in your presence. Help me to concentrate on your goodness and not my concerns. Keep my attention focused on you so that I do not slip into doubt and worry.

Pierce, my soul with your presence. Allow me to feel your faithfulness.

In Jesus' name, I pray. Amen.

Goodness & Grace

Surely your goodness and love will follow me all the days of my life, and I will dwell in the house of the Lord forever.
Psalm 23:6 (NIV)

God, thank you for your goodness and your grace. To know that goodness and grace follow me daily reassures me that nothing I go through is all bad. I love you, Lord, for your unchanging love! Whether it be tough love, agape love, mania, pragma or philia, your love has no end. You love me when I do not even love myself. Your love fights for me when I have given up. Your love steps in when I feel like the person who loved me most left. Your love remains! Your love sustains! Your love has no stipulations, and I am grateful for the opportunity to dwell in it forever.

In Jesus' name, I pray. Amen.

Hope Overflow

May the God of hope fill you with all joy and peace as you trust in him, so that you may overflow with hope by the power of the Holy Spirit.
Romans 15:13 (NIV)

Lord, be the supplier of my hope. Forgive me for placing my hope in promotions, opportunities, and people. Fill my cup of hope when the cares of this world have emptied it.

Burn away my desire to put my hope in anything other than you. Protect my hope and hide it in the depths of your heart. Grant me joy and peace as I place my hope back into you. Hire your Holy Spirit to govern my mind and soul. Hold my hope hostage, Jesus! I declare that hope is returning to me this week!

In Jesus' name, I pray. Amen.

The Good Shepard

I am the good shepherd. The good shepherd lays down his life for the sheep.
John 10:11 (NIV)

God, nobody cares about me the way you do. You will not leave me unattended to fend for myself. You do not hold my disobedience against me. Thank you for correcting me in love. Thank you for not trading me in for the next best thing. Thank you for working with me, waiting for me, and loving me unconditionally.

God, thank you for being better than good. Thank you for taking a chance on me and for sticking it out with me! I am glad you saw fit to save me from my sins. I praise, worship, and adore you for the extra you gave that I did not deserve.

I declare that I will rise to your standards today. I will be better, do better, and produce better for you. God, allow your work ethic, love, and temperance to manifest in my life. Make me more suitable for your use.

In Jesus' name, I pray. Amen.

Patch and Go

As a dog returneth to his vomit, so a fool returneth to his folly.
Proverbs 26:11 (KJV)

Today, I pray that you deny my access to all the places that I have the desire to go that is not like you. Patch up holes that I have opened that allow things to seep in that are not pleasing to you. End this rollercoaster ride of foolishness. End the trajectory of insanity that I have fallen victim to in the past.

I declare that for the rest of my life I will use good sense over common sense! I will not be like the dog that eats its own vomit. I will no longer indulge in the enemy's entrée.

God, patch the holes, close the gaps, and fill the voids. I decree and declare that I will leave the past behind me today.

In Jesus' name, I pray. Amen.

Too Far Gone

Listen! The Lord's arm is not too weak to save you, nor is his ear too deaf to hear you call.
Isaiah 59:1 (NLT)

God, I confess that I am a sinner only saved by your grace. I am not too proud to beg or plea for your forgiveness. Forgive me, Lord, and ensure me that at the end of the day you still love me.

I decree that "too far gone" does not apply to me. I decree a return, a reunion, and a part two to my story! I know that when I disobey, I have to pay. I am not asking for a get out of jail free card but a return to go card. God, I am praying for another chance and another opportunity to do things better than I did before.

Accept me back into your good grace. I pray that you give me the spirit, courage, and humility to endure the results of my sins.

In Jesus' name, I pray. Amen.

No Substitutes

That if thou shalt confess with thy mouth the Lord Jesus, and shalt believe in thine heart that God hath raised him from the dead, thou shalt be saved.
Romans 10:9 (KJV)

Nothing can substitute for the truth. Everything that is written in your word is what will be. No amount of money can get me a fast pass into the gates of heaven. My good deeds, kindness, or philanthropy cannot reserve my spot.

God, I want to make it into heaven! I confess that Jesus is my Lord and savior! I believe that you are who you say you are. God, I believe that Jesus is the way, the truth, and the life as it says in John 14:6.

God, thank you for revealing who you are to me. Thank you for showing me that there are no substitutions for you. Help me to believe still when life is going well or seemingly bad. Help me to stay grounded in the truth.

In Jesus' name, I pray. Amen.

Dressed to Impress

I beseech you therefore, brethren, by the mercies of God,
that ye present your bodies a living sacrifice, holy,
acceptable unto God, which is your reasonable service.
Romans 12:1 (KJV)

God, make me presentable to walk amongst people in your name. Wash me up, remove all the dirt, and intensify the aroma. Take my ashes and give me beauty! Allow the change that I want to see to take root in me first. I decree a new look in the next 30 days, a look that encourages the weak in faith. A look that wakes up the dormant dreamer and believer.

Dress me in unwavering faith. Use me to showcase how your goodness can renew a right spirit within the lost. Advertise your anointing through my willingness. Use my life to impress upon others the importance and reward that comes with following you. Make me the model for your mission!

In Jesus' name, I pray. Amen.

Ignore Ignorance

For anger gives a foothold to the devil.
Ephesians 4:27 (NLT)

Not today Satan! You will not wipe the progress from up under my feet. I have come too far to let this situation get the best of me. God, I have been praying, fasting, and expecting temperance to show up in my life. I decree that restraint is here to stay this week. I will not allow the ignorance of others to control me. I will not let my flesh weaken my faith.

This will not be a week of defeat but of success. I declare that this will not be a weak week! Strength take root in me, right now. I decree 1 Corinthians 15:58 to show up in my life. I will ignore the ignorance that wants to me to sin.

In Jesus' name, I pray. Amen.

Stop Being Fake

A good person leaves an inheritance for their children's children, but a sinner's wealth is stored up for the righteous.
Proverbs 13:22 (NIV)

God, I am going to faith it until I make it! It is no sense in faking something that you already promised to me. I declare that fake is not a part of my story. My legacy demands faith to show up and show out. Fake cannot turn into real, but my faith can transform into results.

God, everything that the devil stole return it hundredfold! I declare Proverbs 13:22 over my life today. I decree that I will not have to steal, kill, or destroy to get back what belongs to me. I do not have to pray on the downfall of something that is destined to fall. I decree a fixed fight in Jesus' name!

In Jesus' name, I pray. Amen.

Consider the Consequences

Dearly beloved, avenge not yourselves, but rather give place unto wrath: for it is written, Vengeance is mine; I will repay, saith the Lord.
Romans 12:19 (KJV)

God, everything in me is telling me to go and handle this situation. The only hold up is my knowledge of Romans 12:19, where you said that revenge is yours. Keep me in line and do not let me fight a fight that belongs to you. I pray that matters do not touch my hands because your wrath is far worse than anything I can convey. Separate me from the trouble God. I pray for a distance between me and the problem and all parties involved. I pray for the "turn the other cheek" strength right now. The devil will not win this way because I know you are here to fight for me.

In Jesus' name, I pray. Amen.

Tap Out

Casting all your care upon him; for he careth for you.
1 Peter 5:7 (KJV)

God, today I cast all my cares on you and I will let them go. For me to avoid damaging myself, I need to place my concerns in your hands. You are the greatest handyman, and you are extremely necessary for my overall being. Only you can provide the means for all of my interests. Forgive me for even attempting to take all these matters into my own hands! I am not equipped to do your job nor do I want to.

God, I give myself over to you today.

In Jesus' name, I pray. Amen.

Prepare Me for Peace

And the peace of God, which passeth all understanding,
shall keep your hearts and minds through Christ Jesus.
Philippians 4:7 (KJV)

God, prepare me for peace today. As peace returns to my life, keep me from reverting to the chaos that disrupted my peace. God, grant me peace but show me how to rest in it. Make peace contagious around my family, friends, and on my job. Mute the noisemakers, gossipers, and complainers. I do not have to know how you are going to do it. I only need to trust that you will.

This week I expect peace and command it to come forth.

In Jesus' name, I pray. Amen.

Mental Health

I will praise thee; for I am fearfully and wonderfully made:
marvellous are thy works; and that my soul knoweth right
well.
Psalm 139: 14 (KJV)

My mental health is not an issue. It was a deciding factor that went into my makeup when you decided to create me. God, you know what I can and cannot handle. You would not give something to me if I were not crafted to care for it. I am confident that you love me and that mistakes are not in your nature. You only bring me to the things you know I can survive. I call a flag on anyone that tries to tell me otherwise.

God, you are better than good. I have my life because you gave up your son's life. Anything and everything that I have will be used for your glory. I decree that I am a glory story! I am no longer embarrassed or angry about any of my God-given genetics. I will embrace who I am and who you are to me.

In Jesus' name, I pray. Amen.

Comfort Zoned Me Out

*What good is it, dear brothers and sisters, if you say you
have faith but don't show it by your actions? Can that
kind of faith save anyone?*
James 2:14 (NLT)

God, I got weary and content in my comfort zone and forgot
how hard starting again could be. Invade my space and push
me out of this comfortable place. Give me the energy to start
again and to try something new. Allow excitement to radiate
through my soul. God, I know that you have much more in
store for me. You have done your part, and I must do mine to
receive my blessings.

I have way more faith than the size of a mustard seed, but I
need help with doing the work. This year I will put in the
work. God energize me with effort. Help me to stop waiting
for the right moment and time. I decree and declare that the
time is now. I rebuke the spirit of perfectionism, anxiety, and
fear that tries to prevent me from starting.

Deliver me from being an observer and make me a doer. I
declare that I will not contemplate when, how, where, and
what to move ahead on but I will immediately follow your
voice. Not my will but yours be done.

In Jesus' name, I pray. Amen.

Recommitted

Obey the Lord your God and follow his commands and decrees that I give you today."
Deuteronomy 27:10 (NIV)

Whatever you want me to do God, I will do it. I tried my way and each time I fell flat on my face. Sometimes I get away with it, and things seem to be going okay. Then, reality sets in - I cannot make it without you! Your ways are much wiser, straightforward, and prosperous. I have caused myself unnecessary misery by being disobedient, prideful, and a know it all.

I do not know half as much as I thought I did. God, today I recommit to you. I recommit to following your guidance over my gut. I recommit to yielding to your way over my way. God, I am committed to doing whatever you want me to do.

In Jesus' name, I pray. Amen.

Forgive Me

Then he said to them, "Watch out! Be on your guard against all kinds of greed; life does not consist in an abundance of possessions."
Luke 12:15 (NIV)

Sometimes I can be greedy! Eating everything and wanting to know everything just always trying to partake in things around me. God forgive me for my greed and for the times I put myself before others because I wanted to be first. Forgive me for being selfish in my desires. I repent for being nosey and overindulging in other people's business.

God forgive me for lusting after life and the things of this world. God, I know you created me to be better. I desire to be better. For the next 30 days, I decree that I will not be greedy but be courteous, loving, and mindful of my desires.

In Jesus' name, I pray. Amen.

Lord Prepare Me

Do not boast about tomorrow, for you do not know what a day may bring.
Proverbs 21:1 (NIV)

Lord prepare me to hear "well done my good and faithful servant." Search my heart and cleanse all my unrighteousness. Wash me clean from all impurities. Forgive me for my sins. God, restore all the areas in my life where I lack your goodness. I repent right now for my sins as tomorrow is not promised. I confess you to be my Lord and Savior Jesus Christ. Move on my behalf right now. Fix my life so I can live in eternity with you whenever you come for me.

In Jesus' name I pray, Amen!

Bless and Release

*Go from the presence of a foolish man, when thou
perceivest not in him the lips of knowledge.*
Proverbs 14:7 (KJV)

Billions of people are in the world! Lord, help me to see that
everyone I encounter is not purposed to remain in contact
with me. I pray that you help me to see that everyone is not
my friend. Keep me from being held up on who supported
versus who did not. Help me to stop holding on to the people
who were only placed in my presence for the sake of passing
by. For those who were destined to teach me something, I
pray I learned the lesson. Give me the strength to cut ties
with people who are strangling me to death.

Today, I pray that you help me to better guard my heart,
space, and time. Make me a better judge of character. Teach
me how to bless and release people with love from my life.

In Jesus' name, I pray. Amen.

Teach Me

My people are being destroyed because they don't know me. Since you priests refuse to know me, I refuse to recognize you as my priests. Since you have forgotten the laws of your God, I will forget to bless your children.
Hosea 4:6 (NLT)

God, I want to know your ways. I want to sense when you are upset, pleased, happy, and disappointed. I want to know everything about you because I want to please you with everything I have. Show me your personality and your pet peeves. I will do anything to behold you as my King. I want nothing more than to honor and bring glory to your name. I pray that my ways are upholding the standards you saw fit when you created me. Teach me to be more like you. Give me your mindset. Teach me to be innovative like you.

In Jesus' name, I pray. Amen.

Follow Suit

Be ye followers of me, even as I also am of Christ.
1 John 2:6 (KJV)

God, I am behind you 100%. I will follow you to the utmost ends of the earth. I will bless others the way that you have blessed me. I will love without conditions just as you love me. I will pray and fast to hear your instructions as you did. I will be the sacrifice as you were. I will take on the hate, criticism, and betrayal because you did it willingly for me. You followed your Fathers plan when it was hard to, and you did not complain.

Forgive me for the complaints that I make. Forgive me for the excuses and the lack of urgency I have when you tell me to do something. Today, I rededicate my life to you, align my life with yours.

In Jesus' name, I pray. Amen.

Advocate Needed

And then he told them, "Go into all the world and preach the Good News to everyone.
Mark 16:15 (NLT)

Life has taught me that people do not hear me the way that I intend for them too. Sometimes the things that I say come off rude, condescending and judgmental. God, I need you to help me become a better advocate for you. I want to better spread your messages of love and mercy without offending others. I pray that you advance my advocacy skills to be better for your use. Impart in me the knowledge, wisdom, and understanding needed to help draw more people to you.

In Jesus' name, I pray. Amen.

Cover My Spouse

Let no one spilt apart what God has joined together.
Mark 10:9 (NLT)

Where there is good evil is always present. God, I come to you in prayer for my spouse. Cover our union in love, loyalty, and honesty. I rebuke the devourer that wants to kill, steal, and destroy what you have ordained. Protect my spouse as they come and go. God, I plead the blood of Jesus over them for the devil will not have this one!

My spouse will be a person after your own heart. They will love, adore, and honor you above all things, including me. I decree and declare that there will be no trespassing in this partnership. God, you are the foundation of our union. I pray that you lead anything and anyone out from around our life who tries to destroy the work of your hands.

Sexual sin, the spirit of lying, hiding, stealing, and manipulation cannot exist here. Family, friends, nor finances can be enough to take us apart. God be the center and the glue that molds us together for your glory.

In Jesus' name, I pray. Amen.

Be Still

Whoever dwells in the shelter of the Most High will rest in the shadow of the Almighty.
Psalm 91:1 (NLT)

Today, I command my mind to be still. God, submerge all my situations with your spirit. Help me to remember that you are God. When things are going in a different direction than I saw fit, help me to trust you. Calm my mind from strategizing how to overcome something you want me to rest in. Today, I will stop worrying about things you are already working out. God, help me to be still.

In Jesus' name, I pray. Amen.

Freedom of Choice

*For you are free, yet you are God's slaves, so don't use
your freedom as an excuse to do evil.*
1 Peter 2:16 (NLT)

Lord, thank you for not forcing me to do the things I do not
want to do. Thank you for giving me a choice in all matters
concerning myself. My prayer is that you watch over me
carefully. Do not let me go too far off without warning. God
ring the alarm when I wander off down the wrong road.
Check me when I do take heed to your instructions.

God, you are always good to me. You always show up when
I ever show out. You never leave me out in the dark without
your light. Forgive me for taking advantage of my freedom. I
pray that you forgive me for running wild and straying away
from you. God, I pray for the wisdom to better manage my
freedom.

In Jesus' name, I pray. Amen.

Risky Resentment

Surely resentment destroys the fool, and jealousy kills the simple.
Job 5:2 (NLT)

"Life's not fair" is what people say to try to make the bitterness go away. However, this is not working for me – bitterness and envy are still chewing away at me. Yes, I know who and whose I am, but the pain of the past still lingers.

God, I am coming to you today for deliverance from resentment. Remove the residue from my mind and paint a new picture within my thoughts. Help me to see that what I thought was the best just was not good enough. Today, I give it all over to you one last time! Today, I will stop replaying the situations that did not go my way. I claim freedom from resentment, regret, and jealous tendencies right now.

In Jesus' name, I pray. Amen.

Temporary Not Eternal

God is our refuge and strength, a very present help in trouble.
Psalm 46:1 (KJV)

Nothing that I have ever been through was too much for me to handle. This situation will not be any different. This temporary setback is a set up for an eternal gain. I am a survivor, and I will beat all odds.

God, thank you for showing me signs and granting me with clarity. Even though I often ignored them, you kept sending signs until I was able to grab hold of them. I pray that I never miss another sign for they are meant to keep me safe. Thank you for staying present when my disobedience was every reason to leave.

God, I feel your presence. I hear you telling me that "it is temporary." I trust you, Lord. By faith, I decree that my troubles will have an expiration date of today! The same troubles from this year will not spill over into the next year. I decree that they will come to an end without ending me, for I shall live and not die. I will reflect your glory, courage, and strength today. I decree and declare that no weapon that is formed against me will succeed.

In Jesus' name, I pray. Amen.

Fix My View

For as he thinketh in his heart, so is he.
Proverbs 23:7 (KJV)

I command today to be an uplifting, prosperous, and productive day. I decree that I will not talk down to myself or others. I will have confidence in myself. I will walk and speak boldly in front of others. God, I will not shrink at the thought of others judging me because their opinion cannot change your opinion of me. I will begin to see myself in the image of you: bold, notable, smart, gifted, and matchless.

Today, I will think better thoughts about myself than I did yesterday! I am already a better version of myself than I was yesterday. God, I know my thoughts are powerful. I pray that you help me to find the positive thoughts in all situations.

I am who I think I am and I will be who I say I will be.

In Jesus' name, I pray. Amen.

Now Faith

Now faith is the substance of things hoped for, the evidence of things not seen.
Hebrews 11:1 (KJV)

God, help me to start having faith right now! I pray that my faith works in my favor today. Bring forth the evidence that my faith is working. I pray that favor follows me everywhere that I go today. Help me to not get frustrated because things are not appearing the way I want them. Help me to press on towards the mark of victory. I declare that the things I am hoping for will be hoped for no more because they are coming into existence right now. I declare and decree that I will see the things I prayed for manifest this week.

In Jesus' name, I pray. Amen.

Balance Builders

So, don't worry about tomorrow, for tomorrow will bring
its own worries. Today's trouble is enough for today.
Matthew 6:34 (NLT)

God, help me to build balance in my life. Help me to be more
realistic with my time and expectations. Help me to prioritize
taking care of myself, spiritually, mentally, and physically.
Help me to be present in my daily responsibilities. I do not
want to miss special moments throughout my day because I
am spreading my focus too thin.

Protect my mind from being overwhelmed and stressed.
Strengthen my spontaneous spirit. I do not want to restrict
myself from enjoying the fun that life has to offer. God, I
believe that you want me to enjoy life and that you want me
to experience new and exciting things. I pray you help me to
find balance.

In Jesus' name, I pray. Amen.

Give Respect

*So, in everything, do to others what you would have them
do to you, for this sums up the Law and the Prophets.*
Matthew 7:12 (NIV)

God, I struggle to give respect to people who do not respect
me. My prayer is that you teach me how to do this. Teach me
how to love people when they have insulted me. Teach me
what to do when my flesh is being stronger than my spirit.
Teach me how to show the same mercy that you extend to me
every day. The same patience that you have with me is the
patience I desire to have in my interactions with others.

I decree and declare that I will show respect. I will give
respect even when it is not given to me. People will not have
the power to pull me out of character. Satan will not steal my
joy. I will control my frustrations and stress. Today, I will put
into practice what I have asked for in prayer.

In Jesus' name, I pray. Amen.

It is Lifted

But you, LORD, are a shield around me, my glory, the One who lifts my head high.
Psalm 3:3 (NIV)

The weight I felt last night has been lifted. The stress that I thought was going to keep me in a negative space has left. Thank you, God, for opening the floodgates of heaven and outpouring stillness! Thank you for keeping a close watch over me this week because I did not think I would make it in one piece.

God, you are the lifter of my head! You lifted all pressure, and now I can breathe again. I can see that you were in this with me all along. Today is going to be a great reminder that you have all power in your hands! Thank you for hearing my verbal and nonverbal concerns. Thank you for stepping in as a caregiver, protector, and friend.

In Jesus' name, I pray. Amen.

Listen

Stop listening to instruction, my son, and you will stray from the words of knowledge.
Proverbs 19:27 (NIV)

God, help me to stop being hard headed. Help me to know when I should learn from experience versus when I should learn from listening. My prayer today is that you help me to understand when to listen. The things in your word are not merely a suggestion or piece of advice.

Your word is the lamp unto my feet, and I need help treating it as such. Humble me and teach me to be obedient. I pray that you help me to adopt the full understanding of 2 Timothy 3:16, which explains how your word is given to help me improve my life. Disobeying you and hoping things turn out right is not how I want to live. Help me to listen more intently to your word and apply it to my life.

In Jesus' name, I pray. Amen.

Spiritually Fit

Physical training is good, but training for godliness is much better, promising benefits in this life and in the life to come."
1 Timothy 4:8 (NLT)

God, I can be overly concerned with my physical appearance sometimes. I have invested time, money, and energy into looking my best. The same amount of effort I put into making sure my physical appearance is good, I want to put towards my spiritual being.

God, show me how to be disciplined spiritually. Help me to be consistent in my prayer life. Strengthen me as I aim to follow your word which feeds my soul. Today will be the start of my spiritual fitness journey. Strengthen me as I seek to strengthen my spirit. Lord, I know that physically working out will never sustain me in the way that you can. Help me to find the balance between being physically and spiritually fit.

In Jesus' name, I pray. Amen.

Old News

Throw off your old sinful nature and your former way of life, which is corrupted by lust and deception.
Ephesians 4:22 (NLT)

Today, I decree that the old me is now old news! No longer will I let people control my behavior. God help me to respond in a new way. In place of pettiness, I will pray. Instead of fighting, I will allow you to fight in my place for me. Instead of defending myself when I am wrong, I will accept correction and move on. God, I decree that my bad habits are old news. I decree that I am a new person because you have cleansed me from all unrighteousness.

In Jesus' name, I pray. Amen.

Whose Next

*Though my father and mother forsake me, the LORD will
receive me.*
Psalm 27:10 (NIV)

Neglect can be a traumatizing experience. It is something that
I do not want to experience again. Neglect from a parent,
trusted family member, spouse, teacher or friend is not easy.
God, I pray that you send people into my life who do not take
their words for granted. When people tell me they are going
to be there for me, I want them to stay. Free me from the guilt
of feeling like I ran people away. Release the anger from
inside my heart. Break down the walls I have built to protect
myself and cover me with your loving arms.

God, I thank you that no matter who left you stayed.
God release people from my life who are on the verge of
leaving. I pray commitment and consistency dwell in all my
relationships for the rest of this year.

In Jesus' name, I pray. Amen.

I Know Better

When I was a child, I spoke and thought and reasoned as a child. But when I grew up, I put away childish things.
1 Corinthians 13:11 (NLT)

I pray for the courage to do the things I know I should and to stop doing those things I should not. I pray for the tenacity to trust in your ability more than my own. I pray that you forgive me for following the devil more than I do your word. Sinning does not always feel bad at the moment. It is easy to convince myself that things "are not that serious."

However, hell and heaven are very real, and hell is not a place I want to go. The best thing is that I get to choose between the two and Lord, I choose you. Forgive me for my spur of the moment sins. Help me to be more watchful as a spur of the moment sin could very well end my life. Today, I declare that I am not a repeat offender. I will not be a backslider. I declare that sin will not win.

In Jesus' name, I pray. Amen.

6th Man of The Year

For just as the heavens are higher than the earth, so my ways are higher than your ways and my thoughts higher than your thoughts.
Isaiah 55:9 (NLT)

God show me where I am needed and where I am not. I want to serve you, spread your love, and help as many people as I can. However, I do not want to overstep my boundaries or outside of my calling. You are God and God alone. I know that you can hold your own.

Sit me down in the areas where I am trying to fill your shoes. I want to support and encourage people to foster relationships with you without me being the focus. I pray that all the people who come to me for help see you and your works through me.

God, I cannot do what you do I can only assist. Place me in the game whenever you need and forgive me for playing out of turn.

In Jesus' name, I pray. Amen.

Secret Weapons

Put on salvation as your helmet, and take the sword of the Spirit, which is the word of God.
Ephesians 6:17 (NLT)

For the next seven days, I will pray the word over my life. God, I will make speaking your word a priority in my daily routine. I will speak the word and most importantly apply it to my life. This week I will work the word. I expect it to take root in me and spill over into the rest of my days. I declare Hebrews 4:12 over me for the next week. I decree that the word will penetrate the depths of my soul and clear out anything that is not of you.

In Jesus' name, I pray. Amen.

Judgement Free

Brothers and sisters, do not slander one another. Anyone who speaks against a brother or sister or judges them speaks against the law and judges it. When you judge the law, you are not keeping it, but sitting in judgment on it.
James 4:11 (NIV)

I repent for being a biased believer. I repent for judging people according to my standards as if my life saved them. Forgive me for not accepting people for who they have presented themselves to be. Forgive me if I was ever the reason why your light dimmed in the life of someone else. God, you do not have favorites, and you love us all the same.

I could be the only light that someone sees and if this is the case help me to stay lit. I rebuke any slanderous spirits that exist within me. Any condemning and judgmental behaviors that cause me to conflict with your word I ask that you take them away. I pray for a loving spirit to override the negative emotions I have towards others who differ from me. God, help me not to judge.

In Jesus' name, I pray. Amen.

Testing, Testing

Examine yourselves to see if your faith is genuine. Test yourselves. Surely you know that Jesus Christ is among you; if not, you have failed the test of genuine faith.
2 Corinthians 13:5 (NLT)

God, thank you for waking me up today! Thank you for a fresh opportunity to practice having faith in you. Today, I want to do a faith checkup. I am anticipating a big move from you, and I want to make sure I am doing my part. God meet me here in this space. Speak to me at this very moment. Speak Holy Spirit for you are welcomed here. By faith, I know that you are here as I can feel you near me. Hear the concerns of my heart.

In Jesus' name, I pray. Amen.

Stepping Stone

But thanks be to God! He gives us the victory through our
Lord Jesus Christ.
1 Corinthians 15:57 (NIV)

Today I will use the devils head as a stepping stone to my victory. Things that seemed out of my league are being granted to me today. God, thank you for turning things around for my good. Today will be the turning point in my life. I declare that the devil set me up to fail, but by faith, I have won.

God, thank you for turning every situation that did not work out for me into a stepping stone. Whenever I felt like I took steps backwards, you were pushing me ahead.

Thank you for not letting my troubles last always.

In Jesus' name, I pray. Amen.

Blind Faith

So, we don't look at the troubles we can see now; rather,
we fix our gaze on things that cannot be seen. For the
things we see now will soon be gone, but the things we
cannot see will last forever.
2 Corinthians 4:18 (NLT)

God, thank you for always being my present help. I am
coming to you in prayer as an interceder today. Things are
not looking too good for my loved one. I have faith, and I
trust in your word, but I am having a hard time seeing past
what is right in front of me. God, be the strength for my
family.

I pray against the spirit of doubt that is trying to drown my
faith. I decree that what I see is not what you see. You see the
sick healed. You see the dying alive. God, you said that if I
have a little faith, nothing will be impossible for me. I am
coming to you with all the faith that I have praying for a
miracle. I may not see the healing, but my faith in you
believes you can perform the healing.

In Jesus' name, I pray. Amen.

For Granted

The end of the world is coming soon. Therefore, be earnest and disciplined in your prayers.
1 Peter 4:7 (NLT)

God, I sincerely want to take the time to thank you for everything you have ever done for me. I thank you for the things you have done for my family and friends. I thank you for all of the beautiful creations that you have made that I get to use.

Forgive me for the times when I took you for granted. Forgive me for underestimating you and for not being completely appreciative of the breath in my body. I am only alive right now because you wanted me to wake up.

While I still have the opportunity, I want you to know that I am thankful. Although, I do not always stop to say this I do love you.

Today, I will not get caught up in my borrowed life, that I forget to thank you for lending it to me.

In Jesus' name, I pray. Amen.

Try Again

Persecuted, but not abandoned; struck down, but not destroyed.
2 Corinthians 4:9 (NIV)

God, thank you for making me unconquerable. Thank you for giving me an undeniable ability to bounce back from the enemies' attack. The power that you placed on the inside of me is amazing. I am humbled at the thought of you extending your sacred power to me as a sinner. To know that you have equipped me with a shield that allows me to go through fire untouched is breathtaking.

With you, I know I can try again. Although I was once persecuted, I am not going to be discouraged or afraid. For Isaiah 41:10 says, that you will not only strengthen and help me, but you will hold me up. I will not fall when I am with you. I pray for the courage to try again.

In Jesus' name, I pray. Amen.

Elect the Elite

But when the time of perfection comes, these partial things will become useless.
1 Corinthians 13:10 (NLT)

God help this world. God, I pray for better candidates to lead us. I pray that you raise up men and women of God to run for offices in your name. I pray that you cover the people who are currently in office. Touch the minds of people who are responsible for making big and little decisions.

God, empower people to vote in ways that will make a positive impact. Forgive us for making a mockery of leadership. Remove people from positions who are not for the people. Cover the ballots from fraudulent votes and place ballots in the right hands. God, I decree that the outcome next year will be better than this one. Continue to cover this nation.

In Jesus' name, I pray. Amen.

DNA

And yet, O Lord, you are our Father. We are the clay, and you are the potter. We all are formed by your hand.
Isaiah 64:8 (NLT)

God, you hold power to change my genetic makeup. What you impart in me no person or science will have the ability to manipulate. I pray that you change the things in my DNA that hinder me from being successful. Remove all the time-wasting toxins in my body. Remove all the fear functions that make me hesitant to shoot my shot.

Place tenacity, dedication, hard work, resilience, and excitement into my DNA. Give me a billionaire's mindset to create, produce and impact. Enhance my spiritual skillsets so that I can live and abound in abundance.

In Jesus' name, I pray. Amen.

Bonds and Bondage

As iron sharpens iron, so one person sharpens another.
Proverbs 27:17 (NIV)

God, teach me to bond with people over our purpose and not
our pain. I will not gravitate to conversations that are
intended to bring others down. I pray that you make me
magnetized for like-minded people. I pray that I will attract
purpose not pain, givers not takers, and supporters not
haters. Make me emotionally available, trusting, and secure.
Free me from the bonds of bondage!

I decree that I will not die at the hand of someone who is
jealous or emotionally unstable. I pray that I experience
healthy relationships with my friends, family, and colleagues.
God help me to make wise decisions when it comes to
making friends. Keep me encompassed around God-fearing
people.

In Jesus' name, I pray. Amen.

Midpoint

I consider that our present sufferings are not worth comparing with the glory that will be revealed in us.
Romans 8:18 (NIV)

God, I am stopping in the middle of my day to pray! I am declaring that the end of today will be greater than the beginning. God, restrain the wrist of the enemy and prevent him from holding me hostage. Keep me strong as I go through the fire. For I know that no pain can compare to the glory you will reveal in me. God, I believe that every middle has an end and I will make it through.
God, do not let me give up in the middle.

In Jesus' name, I pray. Amen.

Compare and Contrast

*Obviously, I'm not trying to win the approval of people,
but of God. If pleasing people were my goal, I would not be
Christ's servant.*
Galatians 1:10 (NLT)

Social media has such a huge influence on the way in which I
see and view the world. I even find myself comparing my life
or life's choices to others. My prayer is that you help me to
use social media for its intended purpose – to connect not
compare. I come against the spirit of detrimental comparison
that makes me second guess my life's journey. I pray against
the spirit of depression and jealousy that can make me miss
out on the joy in my experiences.

God help me to live in the moment and do not let me rush it.
Help me to experience pure joy and happiness. Help me to
use social media in a way that positively motivates others. If
any of my content makes others feel less than, help them to
see that it is through you that I receive my blessings, esteem,
and happiness.

In Jesus' name, I pray. Amen.

White Lies

The Lord detests lying lips, but he delights in people who are trustworthy.
Proverbs 12:22 (NIV)

God, thank you for placing power in my words. Today, I pray for common sense to use my words in an edifying way. Forgive me for the times I have told white lies to escape taking on more responsibilities. I repent for saying "I am broke," or "I am not feeling well" just to get out of doing something when I could have just said no.

God, I pray that you reverse the effects of my white lies. For by your stripes I am healed and all my needs you supplied. Forgive me for lying thinking that I am sparing the feelings of others. Forgive me for disregarding your feelings every time I broke your commandment in Leviticus 18 that says not to lie. God break my habit of telling white lies. I pray that you help me to be honest at all times and not just when it is convenient to be.

In Jesus' name, I pray. Amen.

Quality Time

Does a young woman forget her jewelry, or a bride her
wedding dress? Yet for years on end my people have
forgotten me.
Jeremiah 2:32 (NLT)

God, you are everywhere I am. It is not an excuse not to
spend time with you. My desire for today is to experience the
joy of being fully present in your presence. Mend my mind
with yours so that I can know what you want for and from
me.

Create routine moments of stillness to prevent me from being
on autopilot. I pray for a one on one spiritual encounter with
you daily. God show me how to have moments of mediation
to hear from you. God, I desire to spend more quality time
with you.

Forgive me for viewing quality time with you as a duty
rather than an honor. It is an honor to know you and be
around you. Help me to terminate the time I spend on useless
things. I declare that I will make time to spend with you
today and every day. I decree that our time will be
intentional, uninterrupted, and meaningful above all else.

In Jesus' name, I pray. Amen.

Sit Down

There are many devices in a man's heart; nevertheless the counsel of the Lord, that shall stand.
Proverbs 19:21 (KJV)

God, thank you for being attentive! I know that you had to stop me this week because I would not have been able to stop myself. Thank you for hearing the cries of my heart. I pray that you increase my minds capability to think about what you would do in the situations I face. I repent for making decisions without consulting your word. As bad as it seems you had to sit me down to save me. You had to remind me why you are God.

Thank you for not allowing me to take control. I pray that you help me to keep my mind on you over all matters in this life.

In Jesus' name, I pray. Amen.

Access My Ability

The Lord God said, "It is not good for the man to be alone.
I will make a helper suitable for him."
Genesis 2:18 (NIV)

Good morning, Holy Spirit! I am praying that you send me
an accountability partner today. Access my ability to see in
what areas I need the most support. I confess that I cannot do
everything on my own – you did not create me to. However, I
struggle to ask for help from anyone other than you. God
help me to open my mouth and ask for the things I need.

James 4:2 says that I have not because I ask not. Help me to
stop being prideful. I am asking for the courage to ask for
help. I believe that you have people lined up waiting to offer
their support. I pray that you humble me! Move me to a place
where asking for help does not make me feel weak but
strong. Help me make room for others to be blessed through
allowing them to help me in my time of need.

In Jesus' name, I pray. Amen.

The Pressure

Because you know that the testing of your faith produces
perseverance.
James 1:3 (NIV)

I have a ton of things to accomplish today. My
responsibilities are through the roof, and I must fulfill them
all. I declare that I will complete them without worrying.
God, calm my nerves and spirit. Help me to do what I can
today and deal with tomorrow when it comes.

I will not try to live out this whole week through today. I will
take my time and use it wisely. I bind the spirit of anxiety and
worry. God, help my spirit to strategize on the best way to
accomplish my task. Help me to pray, pause, and plan when
the pressure gets heavy.

I will not give a foot to the enemy this week. I will not even
acknowledge his tactics to take me out. I declare that every
tactic is a test, and I decree that I will pass!

In Jesus' name, I pray. Amen.

Push Through

Let perseverance finish its work so that you may be
mature and complete, not lacking anything.
James 1:4 (NIV)

Today, I will not take the easy way out! I will fight until the finish. Today, I will take every ounce of faith I have to press forward. I will not stop because things are hard I will stop because things got done. God prolong my patience to endure through this week. Today, I will work with the mindset of a finisher with faith. I will grow in confidence and wisdom. I will keep pushing – praying until something happens.

In Jesus' name, I pray. Amen.

No Fear in Faith

Peace I leave with you; my peace I give you. I do not give
to you as the world gives. Do not let your hearts be
troubled and do not be afraid.
John 14:27 (NIV)

Faith and fear will not coexist in my life. God, strengthen my faith to drown out all fear in my life. For what reason shall I fear? Jesus overcame death after being nailed to a cross, and I claim the same strength right now! God give me the courage Jesus had. Give me victory in every war. Fear merely exists to warn me of the things I should not do. I decree that faith will be the filter of my behaviors, not fear. I pray that you keep fear from paralyzing my faith.

In Jesus' name, I pray. Amen.

God or Greed

No one can serve two masters. Either you will hate the one and love the other, or you will be devoted to the one and despise the other. You cannot serve both God and money.
Matthew 6:24 (NIV)

God, thank you for providing me with the means to support myself. No source of income is possible without your authorization. I am grateful to have been blessed with all the material things you provide but God, I desire more of you.

Forgive me for being devoted to the demands of my job and not your word. Forgive me for being greedy in my giving, and for only being concerned with saving for myself. Forgive me for worrying about more when you have already blessed me with enough.

I decree that I will be a generous giver and tither. I declare that I will praise you and not pennies. I pray for knowledge and understanding on how to properly manage the money that I make. Help me to be mission hungry and not money hungry. God, release the greed in me and fill me up with you instead.

In Jesus' name, I pray. Amen.

Moving Me

Guide me in your truth and teach me, for you are God my
Savior, and my hope is in you all day long.
Psalm 25:5 (NIV)

Today, I make the declaration that I am moving forward. God guard my back as I follow your voice ahead. Cover my sides as I go forth with steadfast faith and focus. I will not take my attention off the target of truth.

I pray that just like a baby learning to walk that you move me in the direction I need to go. Pick me up and turn me around when I reach a dead end. Move me from in front of the table of deceit. Protect my innocence from those who want to take advantage of it. God stay with me and keep moving me forward.

In Jesus' name I pray, Amen

Give to Get

Give, and it will be given to you. A good measure, pressed down, shaken together and running over, will be poured into your lap. For with the measure you use, it will be measured to you.
Luke 6:38 (NIV)

God, I am praying that this year's transition does not take a lifetime for me to adjust. Getting used to change is not always easy. I pray that I quickly gravitate to the shift you are sending to me today. God, I trust you with all of me, but the transition of trusting with my finances has been tough.

God, teach me to be the giver that you desire for me to be. Remove my old ways of thinking and give me a new insight into how givers gain. I pray that you speak to me when it is time for me to give. I decree that I will think in a new way, and sow in a better way. You did not create me to be stingy or withhold from those who are in need. I repent for saving everything instead of sowing something.

I thank you for entrusting me with your blessings and for giving me another chance to do right by them. I thank you for transitioning me into a cheerful giver! I thank you for immediately transferring all the grace, mercy, and wisdom I need to go forth in this calling.

In Jesus' name, I pray. Amen.

Friend or Foe

*Wounds from a sincere friend are better than many kisses
from an enemy.*
Proverbs 27:6 (NLT)

God, thank you for releasing me from friendships that were
not real. I thank you for being the example of a true friend. I
appreciate you for exposing the foes now instead of later. I
am truly grateful for the friends I have left, and I pray that
you bless them for the blessings they are to me.

God, bless them for being honest with me when it was hard
to. Bless them for being my confidant and reassurance when I
am down. Bless them for not encouraging my sin but
advising me against it. God, I pray that you give them the
desires of their hearts for fulfilling a desire of mine. I prayed
for some loving, loyal, consistent, honest, and funny friends
and you answered me. Thank you for answering my prayer.
Continue to bless my friendships and use them for your
glory.

In Jesus' name, I pray. Amen.

The Struggle Is Real

Don't repay evil for evil. Don't retaliate with insults when people insult you. Instead, pay them back with a blessing. That is what God has called you to do, and he will grant you his blessing.
1 Peter 3:9 (NLT)

God, help me to be the bigger person. I pray that you train my mind to treat others better than they treat me. God, you called me to bless those that persecute me, and this is not an easy thing to do. You must help me figure out of to do this or I will fail, as I have failed many times before.

Set my pride aside today. I want my entire life to be pleasing to you, and I admit that this is an area where I am struggling. I want to be obedient to your word because I know that it is better to be blessed by you than cursed by you. Show me what being a blessing to someone who is rude and evil looks like because I do not understand.

God, I pray that you just humble my heart. Strengthen my spirit to react out of love, understanding, and not hatred. Change my interpretation of your word so that being the bigger person is not seen as a weakness but as worship unto you.

In Jesus' name, I pray. Amen.

Delete Depression

Anxiety weighs down the heart, but a kind word cheers it
up.
Proverbs 12:25 (NIV)

God, have not created me to worry or fear. So I come against the spirit of depression. I pray that you boost up my physical and emotional strength to function in the way that you created them to. I pray against the spirit of hopelessness and bind up the voices in my head that tell me things will not get better. Things will get better in Jesus' name!

I speak a word of hope over myself right now in the name of Jesus. I speak life, healing, and second chances right now. I decree that my mind is not lost, and I command it to take heed to your word. Depression must flee today! I may not be able to defeat depression but God your word can. Send Christ-like people to speak strength into my spirit today. Anxiety will not overtake me today, and hopelessness will not rest in my heart.

I declare that I am free from depression.

In Jesus' name, I pray. Amen.

No Favorites

Then Peter replied, "I see very clearly that God shows no favoritism.
Acts 10:34 (NLT)

God, thank you for not playing favorites. Thank you for accepting me although my plate is not squeaky clean. Your open-door policy reminds me of just how good you are. Whenever and whatever state I come to you in, you still find a purpose for my use. I thank you for the love and mercy you have shown me because it has made me more confident.

I pray that you help me to honor the open-door policy within my own life. Help me to receive people as they are and not judge them for the troubles they face. Build me up so that I can help build up others. Help me to make others feel loved in similar ways that you make me feel loved. Forgive me for having a favorite type of person or cause to help when you have created me to help all people.

In Jesus' name, I pray. Amen.

Lust After Life

But he will pour out his anger and wrath on those who live for themselves, who refuse to obey the truth and instead live lives of wickedness.
Romans 2:8 (NLT)

God forgive me for living for me. Forgive me for trying to obtain the life that I want to live. Forgive me for putting my fleshly desires before yours. I repent for being disobedient and for not following through on the plans that you gave me to follow. God, remove any selfishness and entitlement from me.

Forgive me for allowing worldliness to rest in the same place as you do. You called me to go into all the world to preach your gospel not to be like the world. I repent for every ulterior motive and hidden agenda in my heart. Forgive me for boasting as your follower when I do not even take heed to your plans for me.

God, give me the wisdom to do your will for my life.

In Jesus' name, I pray. Amen.

Lost and Found

In the same way, there is more joy in heaven over one lost sinner who repents and returns to God than over ninety-nine others who are righteous and haven't strayed away!
Luke 15:7 (NLT)

God, thank you for pointing every sign in your direction. You never left my side, and I love you for that. You knew just when to pause my plans. You pushed me out of my comfort zone and pulled me in when I ventured off. I thank you for the grace and mercy that you placed in my path. I thank you for using others around me to speak to me when I could not hear you for myself. Whenever I was lost, you found me. Whenever trouble blinded me, you helped me to see that you were still in control. God, whenever I find myself wandering around aimlessly for something more, give me you.

In Jesus' name, I pray. Amen.

Pathway to Purity

How can a young person stay on the path of purity? By living according to your word.
Psalm 119:9 (NIV)

God my prayer today is that you cleanse me from all unrighteousness for my soul's sake. Free me from the contamination of sin. Sin is expensive, and I cannot afford to keep living with it. I repent for not living according to your word. Forgive me for following my path and neglecting the one you placed in front of me. Today, I recommit my life to you. I pray for the courage to follow through with what you tell me to do.

Help me to spend more time in your word so that I know what you want from me. Today, I eliminate every distraction and excuse that has prevented me from reading your word.

In Jesus' name, I pray. Amen.

Seek Ye First

Very early in the morning, while it was still dark, Jesus got up, left the house and went off to a solitary place, where he prayed.
Mark 1:35 (NIV)

God, thank you for always being available in the morning, noon, and at night. I pray that you help me to spend more time with you in the morning. Forgive me for allowing my responsibilities to overshadow you. If it were not for you, I would not even have responsibilities. I repent for my negligence.

God, shift my spirit so that it longs for you before anything thing or anyone else. God, you do not have to place breath in my body every day, but you do. I do not take your kindness for granted. I pray that you help me to find my solitary place with you in the mornings. Hide my day's joy, peace, and guidance in the morning. Release your blessings and direction only after I seek you.

I declare that I will find you when I seek you.

In Jesus' name, I pray. Amen.

Patience in The Promise

The Lord is not slow in keeping his promise, as some understand slowness. Instead he is patient with you, not wanting anyone to perish, but everyone to come to repentance.
2 Peter 3:9 (NIV)

God help me to see that I am not waiting for you but that you are waiting for me. Thank you for waiting! Thank you for having self-restraint in your conduct. Thank you for tolerating me through the troubles I cause. Thank you for bearing through my unbelief. I pray that you help me to get myself together before it is too late. Give me the courage to right my wrongs.

Forgive me for rushing you when you were only giving me time to get right. Thank you for not moving to the beat of my drum. God, I pray that when you come back, I will be ready to go. I pray that when you fulfill your promise, I am in the number of people blessed by it. God, show me the areas in my life that you are still waiting for me to get right.

Thank you for embedded patience in your promise. Thank you for waiting on me.

In Jesus' name, I pray. Amen.

Why Me

Consider it pure joy, my brothers and sisters, whenever you face trials of many kinds.
James 1:2 (NIV)

Good morning, Holy Spirit! Today, I pray that you release me from past harm from the hands of other people. I did not deserve what happened to me, and neither did you. We share in the same sorrow caused by pain and I decree that we will share in the same success created by victory.

Victory today is mine! Freedom from flashbacks today is mine. Whatever it is that that devil planted to destroy me - I count it all joy! He planted pain and out grew purpose. He planted deceit and out grew destiny. He planted struggle and out came success. He planted distractions and direction came from it. He planted me in the dark and God you brought the light. I thank for using me as a testimony and vessel for victory.

In Jesus' name, I pray. Amen.

The Inner Struggle

And ye shall know the truth, and the truth shall make you free.
John 8:32 (KJV)

God, I know without a shadow of a doubt that you love me just the way I am. But God, I want you to be pleased with me. I pray that wisdom, knowledge, and understanding flood my mind. I pray for an immediate transformation to take place in my life. Help me to make the necessary life changes that will make you pleased with me. Take desires out of me that are not like you. Release me from bondage and the strongholds of sin.

I pray that I come to know the truth of your word. Help me to make decisions that align with the truth. I still do things I know I should not, and I pray that you help me to stop.

In Jesus' name, I pray. Amen.

Looks Can Kill

But I am not surprised! Even Satan disguises himself as an angel of light.
2 Corinthians 11:14 (NLT)

Dear Lord, protect me from the wolves in sheep clothing. Protect my potential from people who only want to see it destroyed. I pray that you help me to see who is for me and who is against me. No matter how much this truth may hurt, God, I trust that it will not kill me. Warn me when I am on the verge of falling for deceit. Help me to know the difference between sweet and sour when the outer appears the same. I decree that the devil's tricks will not blindside me. I will outsmart Satan, and he will have no control over me.

In Jesus' name, I pray. Amen.

Missing Motivation

*So, dear brothers and sisters, work hard to prove that you
really are among those God has called and chosen. Do
these things, and you will never fall away.*
2 Peter 1:10 (NLT)

God, I need you to motivate me like never before. I pray for
enthusiasm to enter every crack in my body. God, I pray for
inspiration on today. I have goals and dreams, but I lack
motivation. Help me to discover the why in my purpose and
passions. God, I know that you have chosen me for your
glory. I pray that you help me to put effort towards fulfilling
my purpose. Initiate excitement in me again and relaunch the
mission in my mind. God, give me creativity, innovation, and
boldness to make my dreams come true. Help me to see the
end from the beginning by faith. I pray for the faith to trust
the process. I pray for a vision of the victory. I pray that you
help me to act on the things I set out to accomplish.

In Jesus' name, I pray. Amen.

Standing in The Gap

Brethren, my heart's desire and prayer to God for Israel is,
that they might be saved.
Romans 10:1 (KJV)

God, thank you for saving me. Thank you for showing me that
your love has no end. Today, I come to you in prayer for my
family and friends who are not saved. God, as I stand in the gap
between them and you begin to close in.

God, use me to get to them. I pray that something I say or do
encourage them to give you another chance. I do not want them
to be left here when you come back. I pray that you touch their
spirit, provide them with a thirst after holiness and
righteousness. I pray that you reveal to them that you are what
is missing in their lives. I pray against anything that tells them
you only accept perfection. Help them to see that your grace is
enough to cover all of their flaws. Release them from fear,
shame, guilt, and stubbornness.

In Jesus' name, I pray. Amen.

Tell on Him

"No, go back to your family, and tell them everything God
has done for you." So, he went all through the town
proclaiming the great things Jesus had done for him.
Luke 8:39 (NLT)

God forgive me for not sharing my story. You have brought
me from a mighty long way, and you are worthy of my
praise. Forgive me for containing your goodness out of not
wanting people in my business.

Today, I will encourage someone with my testimony. I will
tell about how you create opportunities for me that have
never existed before. I will share how you heal me when I am
sick. You keep saving me from death my sins can cause. You
calm my attitude, nerves, and silence the fear in my mind.
You release me from reaping the consequences of things I do
wrong.

God, you are great, and I will forever tell of your goodness.

In Jesus' name, I pray. Amen.

It's Ended

But if the unbelieving depart, let him depart. A brother or a sister is not under bondage in such cases: but God hath called us to peace.
1 Corinthians 7:15 (KJV)

Today, keep me focused on your promise. God, release me from the pressure of holding something together you want apart. Let me live on in loyalty and love. Help me to see that this end will bring a new beginning. God, give me the sense to know that if someone desires to leave, my role is to let them go. Help me to get it right the next time. I pray that you hold me together, do not let me lose my sanity or peace of mind.

In Jesus' name, I pray. Amen.

Override It

A man's gift maketh room for him, and bringeth him before great men.
Proverbs 18:16 (KJV)

Somebody told me that I cannot accomplish my goal, but I know that you can! Today, I pray for unfair favor. I pray that the greatness of your grace has my name on it. I pray that you make a way out of no way! Stop the struggle and grant the success. Make me an example of what great faith in you can do.

I decree that what took other people decades to accomplish will only take me months. God, you planted this seed in my spirit, water it until it comes to pass! Show up in the system that tries to deny my access. I declare that nothing shall be impossible with you! What man says cannot be done, I claim it done.

In Jesus' name, I pray. Amen.

Lazarus Lived

Jesus responded, "Didn't I tell you that you would see God's glory if you believe?"
John 11:40 (NLT)

Jesus, thank you for reviving the dead situations in my life. People may wonder how I was able to make it through the storm in my life, but I know it was you. I believe that your goodness follows me day in and day out.

Today, I come to you on behalf of a situation that has been dead for years. If you can save Lazarus after four days of death, there is no restriction on the amount of time it will take you to breathe life into this situation again. Dead dreams, desires, opportunities, and relationships I command them to live.

I decree that I will live to see God's glory revealed in my life.

In Jesus' name, I pray. Amen.

Connect to The Source

In vain you rise early and stay up late, toiling for food to eat - for he grants sleep to those he loves.
Psalm 127:2 (NIV)

A pause is not a quit. Taking a break does not mean I broke! God, I need a breather for a re-up of strength. Please end the cycle of insanity that leads me down paths I do not desire to be. I need to rest and refocus. I am praying that you grant me with an intentional pause and a deliberate break.

God, I am tired, but I will not throw in the towel. Remove all worry that keeps me up late at night. I command stress to flee from me in Jesus name. Thank you for taking heed to the heaviness. I declare that today will be a struggle-free day.

In Jesus' name, I pray. Amen.

It Is Meant to Be

The Lord will work out his plans for my life - for your
faithful love, O Lord, endures forever. Don't abandon me,
for you made me.
Psalm 138:8 (NLT)

Today, I decree that what is meant to be is already here!
Everything that I have been praying for is already on the
way. Healing, breakthroughs, miracles, signs, fresh favor,
and mercy will be here by tomorrow. I will not have to seek
advice about this because I believe it is already done. No
counselor or life coach can prepare me for the things you are
going to release.

God, thank you for not being stingy and selfish. Thank you
for not revoking your grace and mercy! I decree and declare
more than enough! I decree and declare new visions and a
new level of faith. I decree and declare that every good thing
with my name on it will be released.

In Jesus' name I pray, Amen!

Rough Day

God blesses those who patiently endure testing and
temptation. Afterward they will receive the crown of life
that God has promised to those who love him.
James 1:12 (NLT)

Today was rough because tomorrow is going to produce
something great. The clarity that will be revealed tomorrow is
going to blow my mind! I decree that four straight signs are
going to point me in the direction of purpose.

God, I feel you moving. I see how you set me up to get me to
this point. The heat I took on today was necessary. The
pressure was purposeful. The cuts I had to endure made me
into who I am designed to be.

People are going to wonder how I made it over. People are
going to want to know how they too can be restored. Give
me the right words to say to point them your way.

In Jesus' name, I pray. Amen.

Blessing in Disguise

I know the Lord is always with me. I will not be shaken,
for he is right beside me.
Psalm 16:8 (NLT)

It did not work out because it was not supposed to. This is not a loss but a lesson instead. A lesson for me to keep my eyes stayed only on you. An experience for me to see that your thoughts are not my thoughts. A lesson for me to remain patient throughout the process. Like bread left in the oven too long, I got burnt. Burnt for trying to be basic when you called me to be royalty. Burnt for leading things on you told me to cut off. God, I learned my lesson. My prayer today is that you turn my lesson into a blessing. Help me to see the blessing in disguise.

In Jesus' name, I pray. Amen.

Cover the City

For where two or three gather in my name, there am I with them.
Matthew 18:20 (NIV)

God, a lot of tragedy is happening in my community. I pray that you watch over all the children in my city. Protect the sources of income that provide stability to the families here. Watch over the city in the morning, noon, and night. Convict the people doing wrong and help them to become productive citizens in the community. Raise up better role models, leaders, and teachers who are prayerful.

Bring forth better education, opportunities, and resources. Secure safe spaces for the elderly. Help the people who are striving to make things better for the city. Enlarge the territory of businesses, churches, and organizations that are making substantial impacts. Send revenue, grants, and donors to help them sustain! Protect our police force within the community. Bring back unity, happiness, and peace.

In Jesus' name, I pray. Amen.

The Family Feud

Bear with each other and forgive one another if any of you has a grievance against someone. Forgive as the Lord forgave you.
Colossians 3:13 (NIV)

I decree and declare that disagreements will not ruin my family. My family will stick together through thick and thin. We will love one another, pray together, and for each other. Money will not come between my family for I pray that we will not experience lack. We will not fight one another only love. Unite us in your deep-rooted love and loyalty. I pray that joy, forgiveness, happiness, and laughter remain in our family.

Sickness and diseases will not flow through generations. I come against every illness, addiction, or malfunction that existed before and I decree no more. I declare that will not gossip, disown, or condemn one another. I decree that we will live to proclaim the works of the Lord. God be the foundation of my family.

In Jesus' name, I pray. Amen.

Kings and Queens

But you are a chosen people, a royal priesthood, a holy
nation, God's special possession, that you may declare the
praises of him who called you out of darkness into his
wonderful light.
1 Peter 2:9 (NIV)

I decree that there is royalty in me! I declare that I am a leader
assigned to lead those who look up to me into the best
version of themselves. God, help me to point people in the
direction you want them to go. I pray that those who will rise
against me in judgment be condemned in love. I pray for
meekness to serve when I have been slandered. I pray that
you bless me with wisdom to use my gifts for your glory. I
pray that the ears that hear will listen. I pray that you keep
the passion burning. Keep my spirit prayerful and my faith
strong.

I pray for the power to keep pushing forward when everyone
in around me is against me. Though I walk through the valley
I will not fear. I pray that you will hide me in your sanctuary
and keep me out of harms reach. I pray that your will be done
here on earth as it is in heaven.

In Jesus' name, I pray. Amen.

Scared to Die

Then Jesus said to his disciples, Whoever wants to be my disciple must deny themselves and take up their cross and follow me.
Matthew 16:24 (NIV)

God, I am nervous about giving my life completely over to you. I am only timid because I know that you are going to stretch me beyond my strength and ability.

I pray that you help me to understand that I am living for you and not myself. My life is not my own. I am not entitled to live it however long or in whatever way I want. Get everything out of me that you ever wanted or needed. I am praying that you help me to live for you.

God, I deny myself today and will follow you.

In Jesus' name, I pray. Amen.

Wild Thoughts

Finally, brothers and sisters, whatever is true, whatever is noble, whatever is right, whatever is pure, whatever is lovely, whatever is admirable—if anything is excellent or praiseworthy—think about such things.
Philippians 4:8 (NIV)

Everything that I do begins with a thought. Every goal accomplished, every decision and sin committed started in my thinking. Today, I am praying for a better think tank! God impart your knowledge into me. Help me to take heed to your warnings. Help me to retain your word so that I can meditate on it. God screen my thoughts and remove anything that would have me to fall into sin.

I declare that my thoughts will not be my downfall.

Today, I am gaining back control over my thoughts. I pray for positive thoughts, and I rebuke negative ones. For your words says in Proverbs 23:7, so a man thinks in his heart, that shall he be. I decree and declare that I will have positive, prosperous, and healthy thoughts.

In Jesus' name, I pray. Amen.

Petty or Prosper

Beloved, follow not that which is evil, but that which is good. He that doeth good is of God: but he that doeth evil hath not seen God.
3 John 1:11 (KJV)

Today, I pray that you humble me in spirit and pinch my petty nerve so that it can no longer operate. Today, I chose to be prosperous over petty. I choose to obey you! I pray that you help me to have self-restraint when I want to act out of sarcasm. Forgive me for allowing my sarcasm to lead to sin. Forgive me for hurting people just because they hurt me. God, I repent for retailing out of hate and not of love. God, mature me and make me over again.

In Jesus' name, I pray. Amen.

Share

And do not forget to do good and to share with others, for with such sacrifices God is pleased.
Hebrews 13:16 (NIV)

God, thank you for sharing your Spirit with me. Thank you for sharing your love and kindness. I pray that you help me to stop being an "every man for himself" type of person. Help me to find the blessing behind sharing. God, help me to see that sharing is caring, not only about the person but you too.

Help me to share in the same manner as you. Forgive me for holding the little I have helped over people's head, making them feel like they are indebted to me. Help me to share freely without wanting any thanks in return. God, I pray that you bless the people who have shared with me over the years. Meet every need they have God.

In Jesus' name, I pray. Amen.

The Warrior in Me

Praise be to the Lord my Rock, who trains my hands for war, my fingers for battle.
Psalm 144:1 (NIV)

God, I pray that you give me your warrior's spirit. Help me to realize the king that is on the inside of me. I pray that you help me to know who I am. Show me the victorious virtue placed in my bloodline. Give me the confidence that you have in me. Speak to me when doubt tries to deter me from going after the win. I declare that I will win every fight because you are my trainer.

God, thank you for making me great. I declare that the battle that is in front of me is not greater than me. I will overcome my problems because you have overcome the world.

In Jesus' name, I pray. Amen.

No Longer

When you were slaves to sin, you were free from the obligation to do right.
Romans 6:20 (NLT)

God, thank you for freeing me from the bonds of sin. Thank you for lighting the way in my path that led me out of darkness. You untangled me out of satisfying sin. Thank you for still saving me when you should have left.

Now that I know what you expect from me I cannot live giving less than my best. Today, I make up in my mind that sin is a waste of my time. I pray that you convict my spirit when my flesh gets weak. Bring back the memories of how sin only felt right at the moment and strengthen me not to be a repeat offender. I pray that you keep me on the path of the righteous.

In Jesus' name, I pray. Amen.

Leaving It Here

For we brought nothing into the world, and we can take
nothing out of it.
1 Timothy 6:7 (NIV)

Dear God, my prayer today is that you help me to leave everything that you placed inside me here on earth before you call me to glory. I pray that all the love that is in me spread amongst the hearts of people who need it. I pray that all the ideas I have will birth into businesses, initiatives, new opportunities, and more to help expand the sphere of your Spirit. I pray that my life is the encouragement for someone else to live theirs.

Everything that I have will be left here on earth when I am in heaven with you. Place my wealth in the hands of people who will use it correctly. I pray that the wealth you give me be enough to last throughout my bloodlines existence. God, I pray that my life is remembered in a way that brings more glory to your name.

I pray that the passion I have for you burn through the hearts of every person I meet.

In Jesus' name, I pray. Amen.

Pay Up

Do not say to your neighbor, "Come back tomorrow and I'll give it to you"— when you already have it with you.
Proverbs 3:28 (NIV)

Forgive me for taking advantage of the people who saw fit to help me when I was in need. Just because a person does not regularly ask for debts owed to them does not rid me of my responsibility to pay. Forgive me for not paying back my debts when I have the means too. God, I pray that you bless the lender double for blessing me.

I pray that you bless the people who I could have blessed and did not out of greed. Forgive me for delaying the blessings of others that you entrusted me to deliver. God, bless me to be a blessing to someone today.

In Jesus' name, I pray. Amen.

Teach the Teacher

The student is not above the teacher, but everyone who is fully trained will be like their teacher.
Luke 6:40 (NIV)

God, you are the best teacher. I come to you today in prayer for our nation's teachers. I pray that you raise up teachers to be in classrooms who were taught and trained by your word. I pray that you assist the school boards in selecting the best candidates to teach our children. I rebuke teachers who want to instill hate, separation, and lies in innocent children.

Protect the children in my family. Help them to retain the things that will help them to excel in life and be standup human beings. Keep teachers with hidden agendas from teaching the children in my family.

I pray that teachers get the respect they deserve. I pray that they earn wages that warrant the success they are instilling in the next generation.

In Jesus' name, I pray. Amen.

Help Me Understand

And he said to the human race, "The fear of the Lord –that is wisdom, and to shun evil is understanding."
Job 28:28 (NIV)

God, I come to you today asking you to forgive me for my sins. Forgive me for all the things I have said and done that were not pleasing to your sight. Help me to learn how to exercise wisdom with understanding.

God, expose all evil in my life. I pray that you convict me when I am unrighteousness. Show me how to shun evil. I pray that you give me clarity on your word. I pray that any controversial topics concerning your word be made clear to me so that I can live in reverence of you.

God, make me bold like never before. Help me to find comfort in my fear of you. Forgive me for being content with evil instead of shunning it. God, I pray that today be the last day I am confused on what holiness is. I declare that wisdom and understanding is coming to me.

In Jesus' name, I pray. Amen.

Help Me to Remember

But when the Father sends the Advocate as my representative—that is, the Holy Spirit—he will teach you everything and will remind you of everything I have told you.
John 14:26 (NLT)

God, help me to comprehend information better. I pray that you help me to retain information that is presented throughout my day. Help me to understand what is being communicated in meetings, classes, and paperwork. I pray that common sense becomes common in my life. I rebuke the spirit that makes me over complicate things.

Help me to be a strategic thinker. Expand the capacity of my mind to understand the things that flow it. Help me to remember your words of wisdom and guidance. Help me to remember all of my commitments and responsibilities. I pray that you help me to exercise my brain cells for your glory and my victory.

I decree and declare that I will comprehend, remember, and obtain information life never before.

In Jesus' name, I pray. Amen.

It Looks Bad

We are hard pressed on every side, but not crushed;
perplexed, but not in despair; persecuted, but not
abandoned; struck down, but not destroyed.
2 Corinthians 4:8-9 (NIV)

Things may look bad, but I will look towards the hills from which cometh my help. God, things may appear ruined, but I know it is just you re-arranging things for my good. Lord be my hero and be my strength. Help me to have a new perspective that produces power in my prayers. I pray that you will enlighten my eyes to see the way that you see.

I pray that you keep me from getting weary at the sight of trouble. I hear you saying "no pain, no gain." God, keep me strong and focus my attention on your promise, not the problem. God, you have never failed me, and I believe that your blood still has power. Cover me, God.

I will stay hopeful and prayerful.

In Jesus' name, I pray. Amen.

You Can't Lie

God is not a man, that he should lie; neither the son of man, that he should repent: hath he said, and shall he not do it? or hath he spoken, and shall he not make it good?
Numbers 23:19 (KJV)

God, I believe that what you said you would do, is done already. There is no need that I have that you cannot supply. I pray that you will keep your promises to me, as I am called according to your purpose in Christ Jesus.

I pray that you protect my heart, my mind, spirit, and innocence from evil thinking. I pray that you give me the patience to wait on you to do the things you said you are going to do. I pray that you wipe away every tear of anxiousness. I pray that you change my perspective on the promise.

I declare that I will focus on how I am going to bless you and how I am going to honor your name for not lying to me. Thank you for being an honest and sincere God.

I decree that the things that look outstanding are going to be outpouring blessings in due time.

In Jesus' name, I pray. Amen.

I am Angry

Sensible people control their temper; they earn respect by overlooking wrongs.
Proverbs 19:11 (NLT)

God, anger is in my heart, and I need you to remove it. I am angry because I allowed myself to fall into the tricks of the enemy. I am mad that I took my eyes off you when all I had to do was listen and follow you forward. Angry that I did not use the power you gave me to fight off temptation. I am upset that I bowed my head when you told me you are the lifter.

I am angry, but I refuse to let the devil win. I decree that I am in control of my temper, and free from anger. I decree that anger will not keep me from moving forward. I forgive myself, and I forgive the others involved. I decree that I will use my God-given sense to overlook the things that used to make me mad.

In Jesus' name, I pray. Amen.

It is Handled

Suddenly there was such a violent earthquake that the foundations of the prison were shaken. At once all the prison doors flew open, and everyone's chains came loose.
Acts 16:26 (NIV)

God, thank you for taking on the things I cannot. Thank you for being a God that is attentive to your fallen children. Thank you for getting me out of situations I do not even know how I got myself in. Thank you for keeping your hand in the situation and not calling it quits.

I thank you for everything you have done. Forgive me for making matters worse by trying to intervene. Forgive me for trying to handle things on my own and prolonging the process for you to move. God, push me out the way and do what you need to do to handle this situation.

Thank you for showing up without delay. Thank you for hearing and answering my prayer today.

In Jesus' name, I pray. Amen.

Laugh It Off

But the Lord laughs at the wicked, for he knows their day is coming.
Psalm 37:13 (NIV)

God, you have an amazing sense of humor. Your humorous spirit is quite refreshing. Today, I pray that you show me how to take on your spirit of laughter.

Today, I will laugh at the trouble that comes my way. God, I know you are on my side. I know that with you I win. It makes no sense for me to worry, fight, or reason with the enemy. God, you look at the enemy as a joke because he is. I claim today to be the last day I waste my energy on the devil. I declare that there is nothing the devil can do that you cannot undo.

In Jesus' name, I pray. Amen.

Treat Them Better

Do to others as you would have them do to you.
Luke 6:31 (NIV)

Today, I will treat others how I want to be treated. God, my prayer today is that you help me to see that this goes beyond my attitude. Treating others well goes beyond just saying thank you and not being mean to people.

This year is my year to train people how to treat me. I am going to sow into people because I want people to sow into me. I am going to be kind to people and surprise them with blessings without them having to ask. I am going to stop getting upset and practice temperance instead.

I am going to give compliments, support, and encourage other people. I will make others feel heard by giving them my undivided attention. I will show more love, understanding, and empathy. I will be attentive to the needs of others and do my best to address them.

God help me to treat others the way that I want to be treated by you.

In Jesus' name, I pray. Amen.

What Now

The Lord will not let the godly go hungry, but he refuses to satisfy the craving of the wicked.
Proverbs 10:3 (NLT)

God, I just took a loss! I am nervous, and I do not know what I am going to do to recover. I feel like no matter how many steps I take forward I am being pulled backward. I want to trust you, and I want to lean on you. Show me what to do, God. Help me to see that there is light on the other side. I feel hopeless, yet I know you are my present help. My time of need is now. I need you, Lord.

God, I surrender to you. I pray that you fix things in my favor today.

In Jesus' name, I pray. Amen.

Washed Potential

See, I am doing a new thing! Now it springs up; do you not perceive it? I am making a way in the wilderness and streams in the wasteland.
Isaiah 43:19 (NIV)

God, I believe in your word. I benefit from your mercy and grace every day. When people looked at me and saw washed up potential they do not realize you were the one who cleaned me. Things may look dead and old to someone else, but I decree that they appear brand new to you. I thank you for not seeing my potential as the past but seeing it in the present.

God, I pray that you fight off the doubt in my mind that tells me I am out of time. God, hinder the voice in my heart that tries to tell me I am working on the wrong assignment. Prove the people wrong who believes that I have already reached my fullest potential.

I believe I am the chosen one destined to turn things around for my family and me. I thank you for sprucing up my potential. Today, I turn my little faith into great faith. I believe that you will do a new thing in me.

In Jesus' name, I pray. Amen.

Command It

For he spoke, and it came to be; he commanded, and it stood firm.
Psalm 33:9 (NIV)

God, thank you for displaying your power in my life. I believe that all power belongs to you. I know that you are powerful and I gain my portion through prayer and declaring your word.

I pray that I muster up enough faith to command things to flee instead of just begging for them to leave. God help me to do things your way so that I can get your results. Today I command victory to show up in my situation. I command mountains of doubt to move out of my way. I command excitement, energy, and enthusiasm to reappear in my actions!

I command my mind and spirit to seek you first in the mornings. I command my hands to put down my phone and pick up your book of power. I command hell to flee from my family. I command my finances to flourish and cover all my expenses. I command Satan to take his hands off me! I command healing to show up and burn cancer out of bodies. I command my God ordained spouse to show up. I command clients, contracts, and opportunities to come forth in my business. I command my debts to be forgiven. I command fear, depressive thoughts, laziness, and bad habits to flee in Jesus' name!

Today, I will stand still and see the glory of the Lord prevail.

In Jesus' name, I pray. Amen.

Battered Believer

And the God of all grace, who called you to his eternal glory in Christ, after you have suffered a little while, will himself restore you and make you strong, firm and steadfast.
1 Peter 5:10 (NIV)

God, you took your beating like the champion you are. You are undefeated, and you win every time. Show me the secret! Show me how to fight like you. I pray that you teach me how to be tough and how to endure to the end.

God, I am a battered believer. I have been hit, beaten, and torn apart. However, I have endured, and I still believe I win. Thank you, Jesus, for your strength to endure. I am still alive when everything I survived should have killed me. I have suffered a while, but I demand that I am restored today.

In Jesus' name, I pray. Amen.

Dumb Decisions

To answer before listening - that is folly and shame.
Proverbs 18:13 (NIV)

God, thank you for waking me up today. Thank you for overriding every poor decision that I have made. Thank you for not causing my choices kill me. Thank you for throwing my sins in the sea of forgetfulness.

Today I come against the spirit of dumb decisions. God help me to slow down! Help me not to rush into something just to get left with nothing. Today, I will consider all the consequences of the decisions I choose to make. I will sit in silence to hear your voice instead of over talking myself.

I decree that the rest of this year will be free from dumb decisions. God enhance my listening skills. Help me to be more attentive to your instructions. I am glad that you call me yours because despite the choices I make you see the good left in me. I pray that you do not let me off easy and keep disciplining me.

In Jesus' name, I pray. Amen.

1 Have a Gift

As every man hath received the gift, even so minister the same one to another, as good stewards of the manifold grace of God.
1 Peter 4:10 (KJV)

Good morning, Holy Spirit it is such a privilege and honor to dwell in your presence today. I come before you asking you to shift my thinking. I am not praying for material things; I just want to know my gift.

I believe that something I have someone else needs and wants. It is in the giving that something becomes a gift. I pray that you help me to see that I have something to offer. I decree that my living is not in vain.

Today I decree that I will discover my gift. I will share my gift with those in need. God, I pray for the courage to be myself because I believe that my gift is attached to my authentic self. I will not conceal my flaws because transparency may make the weak in spirit stronger. God, somebody needs me to be who you called me to be so they can be bold enough to be who you called them to be.

God, reveal to me who my gift is intended to bless.

In Jesus' name, I pray. Amen.

The Essentials

Giving thanks always for all things unto God and the Father in the name of our Lord Jesus Christ.
Ephesians 5:20 (KJV)

God, thank you for waking me up today in my right mind. I thank you for eyesight, for functioning lungs, and for a beating heart. I thank you that I woke up with every essential thing that I need to live. I have food. I have a place to sleep, and my body is clothed. God, I thank you for blessing me with the basics.

God, forgive me for complaining about the responsibilities that come along with the blessings that I prayed for. Thank you for the experience to even know what a bill is. I repent for complaining about bills as someone will never have to worry about bills because they do not have a place to sleep. They do not have a car to drive, and they do not have a phone to communicate on, but I do. God, I thank you for all blessings big and small.

In Jesus' name, I pray. Amen.

Chase God

Seek the Lord while you can find him. Call on him now while he is near.
Isaiah 55:6 (NLT)

God forgive me for chasing after everything besides you. God, I pray that the same speed I pursue after success with be used in my pursuit of you.

Place in me a desire to spend time in your word. I read many books yet struggle to read chapters in the bible. I find time to exercise and attend social events but cannot make it on time to church. God renew a fresh and dedicated spirit in me.

I decree that this week will be a marathon for the mission. I will seek you and study your word.

In Jesus' name, I pray. Amen.

I Obeyed

I have glorified thee on the earth: I have finished the work which thou gavest me to do.
John 17:4 (KJV)

God, I did my part. I did things your way, and I will wait in expectation for your results. God, I pray that you forget not my faithfulness, remember my sacrifices, diligence, and obedience.

Today, I decree that heaven is opening up and blessings with my name on them are being released right now as I pray. Answers to my prayers are coming soon. I decree that finances are overflowing in my account. I declare that yesterday's troubles were disguised as today's blessings. God, I believe that what you create, you care about and I know you are listening.

Move in my life today God. Honor my obedience.

In Jesus' name, I pray. Amen.

Strong Minded

But my people would not listen to me. They kept doing whatever they wanted, following the stubborn desires of their evil hearts. They went backward instead of forward.
Jeremiah 7:24 (NLT)

God, I can be strong-minded at times. Sometimes I do not care who says to go or do something if I do not want to, I will not. God, deliver me from this attitude and stagnant state of mind.

I pray that you help me to release stubbornness. Help me not to be so strong in mind that I neglect to listen to what you tell me to do. God, use my strong-mindedness for your glory. Keep my mind strong when the devil tries to tempt me with temptation. Help me to be strong-minded when the people invite me to do things I know you do not approve.

I pray that you help me to be mentally tough to where the devil sees me as a waste of his time. I decree that my mind is strong when it comes to keeping your commandments.

In Jesus' name, I pray. Amen.

Why Me

And those he predestined, he also called; those he called, he also justified; those he justified, he also glorified.
Romans 8:30 (NIV)

God forgive me for all of the times I questioned you. I pray that you will help me to see that you chose me for this life because I am qualified to live it. You wanted me to be born into this family because it was everything I needed to move forward. You placed me in this job to represent your power.

You gave me these passions to compliment my purpose. My passions are not obsolete, and they are not useless. They will be used to fulfill the purpose you gave to me. When the devil tries to point out what skills I do not have, help me to remember that the ones I do possess are meaningful.

God, you chose me by choice because you did not have to. With billions of people in the world, you decided to give me these specific passions, dreams, and characteristics. Help me to use them for your glory no matter how insignificant they may seem.

God, you knew I could handle the responsibilities and the fire. I pray that you help me to see that I can too.

In Jesus' name, I pray. Amen.

Be the Light

But if you cause one of these little ones who trusts in me to fall into sin, it would be better for you to have a large millstone tied around your neck and be drowned in the depths of the sea.
Matthew 18:6 (NLT)

Good morning, God. I want to thank you for being the light of my salvation. Thank you for shining your light so bright that it caused all darkness to fade. My prayer today is that you help me to not take my light for granted. Help me to remember that someone is watching me, to see if you are real. Someone is watching me just to see if prayer works. Do not let me be the reason a person stops or never starts believing in you.

God, help me to be dedicated to my relationship with you. Help me to be steadfast in the things I boast about believing. I believe you are the only living God. I believe you hold all power in your name. I know you to be a healer, provider, and sustainer. I believe in your grace, mercy, and I fear your wrath. Allow my life to show what I believe.

I pray that you help me to my light lit.

In Jesus' name, I pray. Amen.

1 Am Protected

I give them eternal life, and they shall never perish; no one will snatch them out of my hand. My Father, who has given them to me, is greater than all; no one can snatch them out of my Father's hand. I and the Father are one."
John 10:28-30 (NIV)

God, you are my light and salvation in whom should I fear? You are marvelous, and you are my only line of defense. I do not have to live in fear because of you. I do not have to worry about what tomorrow will bring because you are already working things out in my favor. I do not have to be concerned with the pressure of success because your power is greater and it will keep me. I am grateful to belong to you.

God, you are my bodyguard, and you protect me everywhere that I go. You stand to wait for the enemy to dare lay a hand on me. I am grateful that the devil cannot get any closer to me than you. God, you cover me under the best protection plan life can offer, and that is Jesus Christ.

In Jesus' name, I pray. Amen.

Thirst

The LORD will guide you continually, giving you water when you are dry and restoring your strength. You will be like a well-watered garden, like an ever-flowing spring.
Isaiah 58:11 (NLT)

God, I pray that you help me to have a never-ending thirst for your Spirit. Morning, noon, and night I desire to be in your presence. You are not only what I want but everything that I need.

I pray for a never-ending thirst after your truth. I pray that you quench my thirst the things that will never run dry. I pray that your love, peace, joy, understanding, and compassion never leave my life. I pray for a never-ending thirst after righteousness.

I pray for a thirst after the things that you have designed just for me. Remove any desires that I have that are not in your plan for me. God, satisfy me with you.

In Jesus' name, I pray. Amen.

Steward Mindset

Moreover it is required in stewards, that a man be found faithful.
1 Corinthians 4:2 (KJV)

God, thank you for waking me up today. I know that today will be a great day.

Today, I pray that you help me to become a faithful steward. God, help me to take care of the things you loaned to me. I pray that you help me to use my gifts properly so that they can prosper your people. I pray that you help me to manage the money you have given to me, and teach me to make a profit. Every responsibility that you have let for me, I pray that you help me to fulfill it.

I pray for the mindset of an excellent steward. Give me the maturity, honesty, and integrity of a great steward. Help me to understand that it is through my faithfulness that you grant me stewardship.

God, help me to be faithful.

In Jesus' name, I pray. Amen.

Teamwork

Two are better than one; because they have a good reward for their labour.
Ecclesiastes 4:9 (KJV)

God between you, Jesus, and the Holy Spirit there is no better example of how a team should work together. I pray that you help me to become one with my teammates. Help me to be a good leader and follower when necessary. God, I want to be an asset to my team. I decree and declare that I will be a motivator, protector, and prayer warrior for my team.

God, help me to find my place on the team. I decree that I will not be a stunt to my teammate's growth. God help me to be driven by passion and not praise. Everyone will not always celebrate my achievements, help me to be okay with that. God, I pray that you strengthen me in the areas that I am weak.

Today, I bind the spirit of split teams. We will work together as one. I decree that together everyone will accomplish more. I call forth unity and victory.

In Jesus' name, I pray. Amen.

Heartless

The second is this: Love your neighbor as yourself. There is no commandment greater than these.
Mark 12:31 (NIV)

God, make my heart more like yours. Your heart is pure, caring, and forgiving. I pray that you remove all the heartlessness from me.

Make me a server, not a savage. Teach me how to care for the needs of others and not just myself. I repent for only caring about myself and not others. You said in your word that if I do not care about your people, I do not care about you. God, I care about you more than anything. Forgive me for being heartless and selfish.

I tried to protect myself from hurt and closed my heart off from others. God, forgive me for treating you like you are not capable of protecting the heart you gave to me.

In Jesus' name, I pray. Amen.

Stop Complaining

Do all things without murmurings and disputings.
Philippians 2:14 (KJV)

God, how did you do it? How did you take all hell, lies, beatings, and betrayal from people and not complain? God, I pray for a spirit like yours.

Help me to get to the root of my complaints. God, you are the ruler of the world. I am your child, you love and care about me. I have no reason to complain. Forgive me for complaining when I can find something to be thankful for instead.

I rebuke the spirit of complaining. I pray for a spirit of gratitude and humility. Nothing that I will go through is all bad - help me to look for the good.

God, when I complain I reveal the lack of trust I have in you. Help me to trust you more. Help me to strengthen my faith in challenging times.

In Jesus' name, I pray. Amen.

Knock Out Nervousness

Such confidence we have through Christ before God.
2 Corinthians 3:4 (NIV)

God, I come to you sincerely asking you to knock the
nervousness straight out of me. If I do not believe in myself,
no one else will.

Today, I will not allow nervousness or anxiety to steal your
glory. I will not be nervous when the spotlight is on me. I
bind the thoughts of failure that I have subscribed to in my
mind. Drive out the nervousness with peace and confidence.

Proverbs 12:25 says that anxiety weighs down the heart, but
kind words cheer it up. God, speak words of life over me
whenever I am nervous. Whisper words of encouragement to
me so that I do not feel alone.

I pray that you help me to focus on the impact I can make
and not my insecurities.

In Jesus' name, I pray. Amen.

Standing on The Promises

Through these he has given us his very great and precious promises, so that through them you may participate in the divine nature, having escaped the corruption in the world caused by evil desires.
2 Peter 1:4 (NIV)

God your promises led me out trouble, only because I followed them. Thank you for honoring my obedience. It is only because of you am I able to pray today. I thank you for your promises because they spared my life.

I have strength because I believed Isaiah 40:29 when it said that you would give strength to the weary. I am free from worry because I thanked you every time I wanted to complain. I am hopeful because Jeremiah 29:11 tells me that your plan is to prosper me and not to harm me. I am wiser, because your word became life unto my soul. I am righteous because you rescued me and hid me from all harm as Psalms 121:7 said you would.

I will forever stand on your promises because I know they are true.

In Jesus' name, I pray. Amen.

Keeping Me Alive

The LORD will preserve him, and keep him alive; and he shall be blessed upon the earth: and thou wilt not deliver him unto the will of his enemies.
Psalm 41:2 (KJV)

God, thank you for keeping me alive. As I reflect on where I have been, it had to be you pulling me through. Forgive me for not seeing sooner that you were my sustainer. I have placed credit in a lot of other places, but the victory belongs to you. I give it all to you because you are amazing God.

When I thought, I lost my mind – you breathed sense back into it. People prayed on my downfall, and you kept me from falling. Thank you for preserving me. I could have been another fallen soldier, but your strength reached me.

I pray that you continue to keep me alive.

In Jesus' name, I pray. Amen.

Let Love Shine

Better is open rebuke than hidden love.
Proverbs 27:5 (NIV)

True love is not concealed or hidden. God, I thank you for loving me publicly. You are not ashamed to love me, and I appreciate that. I never have to question your love because you love out loud. Anchor my soul in love. Without love I am nothing, and I gain nothing.

Today, I will not be ashamed or hesitant to tell people I love them. I will not fear the responsibility that comes with loving someone. God, help me to express love throughout my interactions. Teach me to love my enemies as well because love keeps no record of wrongdoings.

God write 1 Corinthians 13 on my heart to remind me that one of my greatest responsibilities is to love.

In Jesus' name, I pray. Amen.

First Place

So, the last shall be first, and the first last: for many be
called, but few chosen.
Matthew 20:16 (KJV)

Good morning God, I will not be before you long today. I just
want to thank you for blessings me with life once more. I
command today to be a great day because you are a great
God! I praise you in advance for the miracles you are making
on my behalf.

God, I believe that being last, will not last always. I declare
that today is my day to be first. Bring forth everything that
you have in store for me.

In Jesus' name, I pray. Amen.

Thank You, Thank You

In everything give thanks: for this is the will of God in
Christ Jesus concerning you.
1 Thessalonians 5:18 (KJV)

I did not reach my goal, but I come to say thank you because I
am almost there. I may not be feeling my best today, but I
thank you for allowing me to be alive. My debts maybe high,
but I choose to thank you because they are going to get low.
The results I wanted did not come back, but I thank you for
the experience.

God, today I am going to condition my mind to be thankful.
No matter what the situation may be, I am going to thank
you. Thank you for still caring about me. Thank you for
easing the pain. Thank you for restoring my heart. Thank you
for being better to me, than I am to you.

In Jesus' name, I pray. Amen.

The Planted Seeds

*Another parable put he forth unto them, saying, The
kingdom of heaven is likened unto a man which sowed
good seed in his field.*
Matthew 13:24 (KJV)

God, thank you for blessing me with millions of good seeds.
Thank you for allowing my seeds to fall on good ground. I
pray that no seed of mine goes wasted. God, bless me with
fertile faith. Allow everything that I touch to prosper. Allow
every seed that I plant to harvest. God, show me where and
when to sow. Thank you for removing all the hesitation I
used to feel when it came to sowing.

Thank you for giving me a sowers heart. I know that every
seed I receive is because I sowed. I pray growth over every
planted seed. I speak life to them in Jesus' name. Seeds go,
grow, and bring me my harvest!

In Jesus' name, I pray. Amen.

Prepare for The Gain

Then I will give you rain in due season, and the land shall yield her increase, and the trees of the field shall yield their fruit.
Leviticus 26:4 (KJV)

Good morning, Holy Spirit. I pray that you have your way in my life today. Be with me and keep me. God, align my life with your decrees. Send the rain and prepare me for the gain. Prepare me for the profit and do not let me be ashamed. I pray as Jabez prayed in 1 Chronicles 4:10, bless me indeed and enlarge my territory. Keep your hand on me so that evil cannot harm me.

God, I thank you for sending the rain.

In Jesus' name, I pray. Amen.

Save The Day

*This is the day which the Lord hath made; we will rejoice
and be glad in it.*
Psalm 118:24 (KJV)

I have already made up in my mind that today is going to be
a good day. I believe that joy is going to meet me everywhere
I go. I believe that peace is already pushing me through
today's problems. God, I pray that your favor follows me.

No matter what today brings, I will declare that this is the
day that you have made. I will rejoice and be glad in it. I will
carry gratefulness and hope in my heart today. I declare that
come what may; you will save the day.

In Jesus' name, I pray. Amen.

Traveling Mercies

Blessed shalt thou be when thou comest in, and blessed shalt thou be when thou goest out.
Deuteronomy 28:6 (KJV)

God, thank you for protecting me as I come and go. For steering my wheel in the direction of safety. For keeping your eyes on the road when mine were elsewhere. God, I thank you for the different methods of transportation which allows me to travel.

I thank you for the planes, pilots, and passengers that make it possible for me to fly. Thank you for keeping me through life's turbulence. Thank you for being the dispatcher that guides me. God, thank you for keeping me safe. I decree and declare that wherever I go, and however I chose to go, I will be kept safe.

In Jesus' name, I pray. Amen.

I Am Ashamed

However, if you suffer as a Christian, do not be ashamed,
but praise God that you bear that name.
1 Peter 4:16 (NIV)

God, I want to thank you for restoring me. Thank you for snatching me from the snares of sin. I appreciate you for covering my flaws and mistakes. I pray that you remove all shame from me. I decree that I will boast about my blessing. I will share my testimony in truth, and I pray that it blesses others. Help me, to be honest, and transparent about the way you have restored my life.

I cannot conceal your clean up. I pray that you help me not to be ashamed of my past. Help me to stay gracious and excited about you covering it and giving me a new start.

In Jesus' name, I pray. Amen.

Say Less, Have Less

My mouth will tell of your righteous deeds, of your saving acts all day long – though I know not how to relate them all.
Psalm 71:15 (NIV)

God, you told me that I could have whatever I say. I pray for the faith to speak the things you want me to have. People may not want to hear what I have to say, but you do. I decree that when I speak, you will listen.

Thank you for always being concerned and attentive to the things I decree. I pray that you help me to use my voice for your glory. Allow me to use my voice to expand your kingdom. I pray that you allow me to use my voice to advance my career. I will say more so that I can have more. I refuse to let the cares of the world to silence me. I declare that my expectations, dreams, and standards are attainable through you.

I will share your goodness. For as I share someone is getting the confidence to approach your throne for themselves. I will not shut my mouth just because others shut theirs. I declare that I shall have whatever I say.

In Jesus' name, I pray. Amen.

Seasons & Reasons

Nevertheless, each person should live as a believer in whatever situation the Lord has assigned to them, just as God has called them. This is the rule I lay down in all the churches.
1 Corinthians 7:17 (NIV)

Good morning, Holy Spirit I would like to thank you for this season you have me in. I thank you for giving me space to myself that allows me to hear from you. I believe that you have me in this season on assignment. God, do not let me miss the mark.

Help me to focus on who I am becoming during this season. This season is strengthening me and preparing me for greater. I thank you for the trials and errors. I will not live in isolation or feel alone for you are with me. I claim happiness in this season. I declare that clarity and growth are taking place in this season. God, stretch when I am too afraid to stretch myself.

I am becoming wiser, wealthier, and more successful in this season. God, help me to stay focused and do not let me rush the process.

In Jesus' name, I pray. Amen.

Examples Exist

Don't lord it over the people assigned to your care, but lead them by your own good example.
1 Peter 5:3 (NLT)

God, I thank you for the influence that you have allowed my life to have on others. I know that there is at least one person who looks up to me. Help me to be a good example for them. I pray that you help me to live in a way that is pleasing to you so they can follow suit.

Make me an example of your glory. Allow my life to be a testament to your goodness. I decree that my Godly influence will stick with people more than their worldly influences. I pray that you bring forth more examples of your power through people in this world. Raise up men and women who believe in your word and live by it.

I pray that Godly examples of men and women are not the last of a dying breed. I decree that we are powerful, successful, loyal, and honest. I decree that we have pure intentions and are in high places with authority to pull others up and to not tear them down.

In Jesus' name, I pray. Amen.

Direct My Destination

We can make our plans, but the Lord determines our steps.
Proverbs 16:9 (NLT)

God, order my steps. Please lead and guide my decisions and my life's journey forever. I do not want to be where you are not. Show me the way that leads to you. I do not only want to find my destination, but I want to enjoy the route. Keep me focused and faithful.

God, I thank you for giving me free will to plan and pursue my goals. I give you my plans and ask that you direct my steps. Take me where I need to go for me to grow. Remove the dead ends from my journey and provide me with new possibilities every day. Allow me to experience whatever is needed for me to exceed the enemy's expectations of me.

I will praise, pray, and depend only on you to see me through.

In Jesus' name, I pray. Amen.

Reveal the Mission

These are the things God has revealed to us by his Spirit.
The Spirit searches all things, even the deep things of God.
1 Corinthians 2:10 (NIV)

Father God, in the name of Jesus, make known to me my purpose and assignment on this earth. I want to fulfill my destiny and be pleasing in your sight. God, speak to my spirit. Reveal the depths of your heart in my mind. Share your secrets with me. Help me to learn everything that you want me to know. I declare that I can go anywhere and accomplish anything because there is nothing I cannot learn.

Uncover your mission and keep it in the forefront of my mind. I pray each day I see your steps leading me in the way I should go. Help me to follow you.

In Jesus' name, I pray. Amen.

A Faded Vision

And the Lord answered me, and said, Write the vision, and
make it plain upon tables, that he may run that readeth it.
Habakkuk 2:2 (KJV)

Father, you instructed me in your word to write down my
vision so that anyone can read and tell others about it. Continue
to inspire me with dreams and hopes that will remain to help
others. I believe that the visions for my future are coming to
past. The fruits of my labor will bless generations to come. For
the visions are not for me but for you to get the glory.

God, I bind the spirit of forgetfulness and blurred visions. The
visions are clear, and they will remain that way. God, write your
visions in my mind and on my heart. I pray that you help me
not to forget them. No matter what things look like now, I will
not allow it to hinder what I believe you told me. I decree that
my visions are vibrant. I declare that they will not fade with
time.

God, impart to me the discipline to work my visions until they
come to pass.

In Jesus' name, I pray. Amen.

Cut All Ties

No, dear brothers and sisters, I have not achieved it, but I focus on this one thing: Forgetting the past and looking forward to what lies ahead.
Philippians 3:13 (NLT)

Father, you said in your word that you know what I need before I even ask. You told me to forget the past and behold the new things that are springing forth. I pray that the new things bring a new level of focus and discipline.

Today, I am cutting all ties with the past as I watch you produce better things in my future. I decree that no past wrongdoing will replay in my mind. No recent sorrow or pain will live in my heart because you are making all things new.

Today, I am moving forward in victory. Thank you, Jesus, for peace, patience, and the promise.

In Jesus' name, I pray. Amen.

Hide Me

Keep me as the apple of your eye; hide me in the shadow of your wings.
Psalm 17:8 (NIV)

God, your word said in the day of trouble you would hide me in your shelter. I take comfort in knowing that I can find safety in you. The quietness of your peace and presence gives me joy. God, even when I feel alone, your presence is with me.

I pray that you hide me from anything and anyone that wants to use, kill, steal or destroy me. Hide me so that the only way I can be found is through people first seeking you. God, box out the enemy that tries to invade my space with worry, gossip, and stress. Be my tower of strength today and every day.

In Jesus' name, I pray. Amen.

Standing Still

He says, "Be still, and know that I am God; I will be exalted among the nations, I will be exalted in the earth."
Psalm 46:10 (NIV)

God, I will obey your word today. I will put my trust and faith in you. I will be still for I know that you are God. I will put my hope in you for you are in control. For your ways are higher, better, and more efficient than mine could ever be. God, I know that you will never fail.

Forgive me for moving without you. Forgive me for taking two steps ahead when you only needed me to stand still. Forgive me for speaking out of turn when my job was to be silent. Forgive me for switching my view when my view should have stayed on you.

I decree that my circumstances will not shake my faith anymore. I declare that I will not stumble or fall because of my situations. I will trust your progress and plan.

In Jesus' name, I pray. Amen.

Catch Me

So, if you think you are standing firm, be careful that you don't fall!
1 Corinthians 10:12 (NIV)

God, catch me and do not let me fall again. I put my confidence in you and not in my strength. You will not let me the cares of the world overtake me. You will not even allow my fleshly desires to control me. God, you are faithful, and you will not let me be tempted beyond what I can bear. You are my way of escape regardless of if I put myself in harm's way.

God, thank you for picking up my slack. Thank you for catching me in the middle of my mess. I know I would not be here if you did not rescue me from falling. I would not have become the person I am if you did not chase after me. You spoke to my spirit and soul even in my sin. Thank you for speaking to me when I tried to run from your voice. Thank you for being persistent and providing my way out.

In Jesus' name, I pray. Amen.

The Middle Man

So, because you are lukewarm – neither hot nor cold – I am
about to spit you out of my mouth.
Revelation 3:16 (NIV)

People say that there are two sides to every story. God, I believe that your story only has one. You are the way, the truth, and the light. Help me to stop straddling the fence and living in the gray. God, you created me to walk boldly not to tread lightly. You gave me access to your confidence through faith.

Forgive me for trying to play the middleman. I repent for loving the things of the world and accepting it as truth. You did not create me to be the commentator between flesh and faith. You created me to trust in you. God, use me as a vessel for your glory. I am with you and not against you. I believe your story is true.

In Jesus' name, I pray. Amen.

Strength to Leave

He giveth power to the faint; and to them that have no might he increaseth strength.
Isaiah 40:29 (KJV)

God, I come to you today in search of an outpour of your strength. Strengthen me to leave the things that are holding me back. God lead me out of jobs that you designed only as placeholders. I pray for courage to step out on faith. You told me not to worry about anything but to pray instead. I thank you right now for the new window of opportunity that is coming just for me.

Give me the courage to leave relationships that are not ordained by you. Strengthen me to stop holding on to unhealthy habits and addictions. I pray that you help me to separate from sin. Strengthen me to depart from the things that make me deaf to your desires.

In Jesus' name, I pray. Amen.

I Am Not Confused

Consider what I say; and the Lord give thee understanding in all things.
2 Timothy 2:7 (KJV)

Good morning, God. Thank you for not being a God of confusion. Your clarity clears up my mind when my spirit is torn. Help me to stop second guessing things. I pray that you make me sober-minded so the devil cannot manipulate me with confusion.

God, I cry out to you for understanding in all things. Bring clarity to my life. Bring direction through your word that I may understand which way to go. You said in your word that you do not change. Now I know that if I ever make a wrong decision, you will still be there with me to redirect me. Help me to find confidence in understanding this.

In Jesus' name, I pray. Amen.

1 Confess

People who conceal their sins will not prosper, but if they confess and turn from them, they will receive mercy.
Proverbs 28:13 (NLT)

God, thank you for being kind towards me. Sometimes it seems unreal how much you care. Forgive me if I ever doubted or questioned if you were real. Today, I confess that I am a sinner only saved by your grace. I admit to doing things wrong when I knew right. Forgive me for being a liar, thief, manipulator, and cheater. Forgive me for being more comfortable in fear than in faith.

I confess for believing that my flesh would flourish me. Forgive me for thinking my ways were better than yours. I repent for rushing your process. Forgive me for being selfish and for mistreating people.

I come to you today as a sinner in search of grace and mercy. Forgive me, God, for I have sinned against you.

In Jesus' name, I pray. Amen.

Comfort Me

"Comfort, comfort my people, says your God."
Isaiah 40:1 (NLT)

God, I come petitioning for your presence to pierce through my soul. I long to dwell in your presence of peace and power. Nothing in this world can take your place in my life. I pray that your unfailing love will comfort me today. Send people into my life who can help in facilitating the comfort you provide.

I pray that you minimize my moments of discomfort. Help me to go through the fire untouched. Strengthen my mind to think of affirming thoughts to prosper me and not to fail me.

I decree that today brokenness and self-blaming is a thing of the past. Suicidal and depressive thoughts cannot rest in my mind or spirit. I will not hinder myself from help anymore. God comfort me at all times.

In Jesus' name, I pray. Amen.

Dethrone

God reigns over the nations; God is seated on his holy throne.
Psalm 47:8 (NIV)

God, dethrone the devil. Allow trouble and temptation to pass over me. I pray for a day of peace, purpose, and love. I pray that miracles, blessings, and joy show up in my life today.

Cover me so that I cannot be found by Satan, by disappointments, or sin. Today, I am going to be productive. I am going to move closer to my destiny. Today, I will not be bothered by anything that is not of you. God, alternate the devil's plan.

You sit upon the throne, but you are not stuck there. I believe that your power is going to come down and protect me today. Your power is going to move in my dreams and bring them forth today. I pray that you reveal your glory through me today.

In Jesus' name, I pray. Amen.

Humbleness

For those who exalt themselves will be humbled, and those who humble themselves will be exalted.
Matthew 23:12 (NIV)

God, I know that you are on the move. I know that you are up to something great because I can feel it in the atmosphere. God, my prayer is that you humble me before you bless me. Allow me to remember my past so that I can stay diligent in my future works.

God, as you send the money, resources, and influence send your grace to keep me sane. I bind the spirit of boastfulness, pride, and entitlement that consumes so many people today. God, protect me from getting big-headed. God, as my account grows do not let my head do the same. For your word says blessed are the meek, for they will inherit the earth, Matthew 5:5.

I believe an inheritance of earthly riches is coming to the just as it says in Proverbs 13:22. I pray that you help me to stay ready so do not have to get ready when it comes.

In Jesus' name, I pray. Amen.

Help Me to Forgive

Therefore, if you are offering your gift at the altar and there remember that your brother or sister has something against you, leave your gift there in front of the altar. First go and be reconciled to them; then come and offer your gift.
Matthew 5:23-24 (NIV)

God, help me to forgive in the same way that you forgive me. Forgive me for making others suffer at the hand of my unforgiveness. Sometimes forgiving people is a struggle. Sometimes I hold grudges and want others to feel the same hurt they caused me.

God, I know that I can be better than this. I pray that forgiving someone becomes easier. Release the unforgiveness in my heart so that you can receive my prayers. God, you forgive me so I know that I can find it in my heart to forgive others. Today, I take back the power I have given Satan. I declare that I will forgive others. Free me right now from the unforgiveness in my heart.

In Jesus' name, I pray. Amen.

Be Better

The one who gets wisdom loves life; the one who cherishes understanding will soon prosper.
Proverbs 19:8 (NIV)

God, help me to become a better version of myself today. Help me to fall in love with who you are molding me to be. I pray for a spirit of excitement and enthusiasm in Jesus' name. I will be excited about who I am and what I have to offer. Remove any desire that I have to be anything other than who you called me to be.

God, give me the confidence to live in my truth. Thank you for not making me a duplicate. God, use my skills to expand your kingdom. I pray that you help me to be the best version of myself this year because everyone else is already taken.

In Jesus' name, I pray. Amen.

Distinctive Discernment

I urge you, brothers and sisters, to watch out for those who cause divisions and put obstacles in your way that are contrary to the teaching you have learned. Keep away from them.
Romans 16:17 (NIV)

God, help me to be more sensitive to your voice. Warn me when I am headed in the direction of trouble. Help me to be attentive to your spirit so that I will know whose advice to accept and whose to reject. I pray that you keep me from being blind-sided by fake people. Keep me in the company of genuine people who encourage me based off of your word.

God, teach me how to watch out for myself. Teach me how to guard my heart and mind in a better way. God, keep your word at the forefront of my mind. I declare that I will know your true word for myself and no one will be able to alter its meaning in my mind.

I pray that you show me how to remove the obstacles that I have allowed others to place in my way. Help me to take what they meant for bad and use it for my good. I decree and declare that my discernment will keep me in the safety of your presence no matter where I go.

In Jesus' name, I pray. Amen.

Better with Time

Therefore we do not lose heart. Though outwardly we are wasting away, yet inwardly we are being renewed day by day.
2 Corinthians 4:16 (NIV)

God, the older I get, the more difficult it seems like things become. Deaths, bills, body aches, and many things appear harder to handle. But God, I know that you are the same today as you have been before. You never change, and your word does not either. I know that the promises I stood on years ago are the same ones that helped me see today. Your power still works.

Today I serve notice on the devil! I decree and declare that power is still in your hands. No weapon that forms against me shall prosper. God, thank you for remaining the same. No matter what age or stage I am in, I declare your power is powerful. I decree that Proverbs 16:31 applies to me, as it states that the gray head is a crown of glory found in the way of righteousness.

God, I thank you for the wisdom and strength you have helped me build over the years. I pray that with long life you continue to satisfy me.

In Jesus' name, I pray. Amen.

Match the Mercy

Be ye therefore merciful, as your Father also is merciful.
Luke 6:36 (KJV)

Today, I will show myself some mercy because I am not perfect. God, your grace, and mercy are enough to look past my past. Show me how to extend this same kindness and forgiveness to myself.

Today, I forgive myself for holding me to a standard above what you expect from me. God, you do not expect me to be perfect you expect me to repent when I do wrong. You expect me to forgive myself and others. You expect me to live in reverence to your name not subjection to myself. God, thank you for being merciful to me. I pray that you show me how to extend that same mercy to myself.

Help me to stop being hard on myself. Show me how to strive for excellence instead of perfection.

In Jesus' name, I pray. Amen.

Look Back

So, all of us who have had that veil removed can see and reflect the glory of the Lord. And the Lord – who is the Spirit – makes us more and more like him as we are changed into his glorious image.
2 Corinthians 3:18 (NLT)

God, as I sit to reflect today, I cannot help but notice how far you have brought me. I am better than I was in the past. Now, I can see you working through me. I experience you in my alone time and through my interactions with others.

I am more confident, bold, smart, and sensible. My attitude is finally in your control. Things that use to make me made do not even hold my attention for too long. I exercise temperance, patience, and I forgive. The troubles in my life taught me to trust, listen, and value you more. I do not shy away from my responsibilities I step up and own them now. The fact that I am alive and well today is proof of your power.

I declare that taking the time to reflect back will carry me forward today. Now that I have enough strength to weather any storm I am more courageous. I see that I can press past pain and aim for my purpose. God, I see that you are my light and salvation. I see that your love is patient, kind, and keeps no records of my wrongdoings.

God, I thank you for showing me my past does not plan my future.

In Jesus' name, I pray. Amen.

You Saw Me

For mine eyes are upon all their ways: they are not hid from my face, neither is their iniquity hid from mine eyes.
Jeremiah 16:17 (KJV)

God, thank you for paying attention. Thank you for seeing that I was broken, lost, and troubled without you. I thank you for recognizing that I needed you. Forgive me for making sin my outlet instead of prayer.

You saw every step I took before I made it. Your love awaited my arrival at every destination, good or bad. Thank you for placing forgiveness at every turn. Thank you for not bending the rules for me but for disciplining me when I needed it. Your tough love brought me back to you.

Thank you for not letting me go unpunished. It pushed me into the person I am today. I pray that you keep watching over me.

In Jesus' name, I pray. Amen.

It's A Yes

For no matter how many promises God has made, they are
"Yes" in Christ. And so through him the "Amen" is spoken
by us to the glory of God.
2 Corinthians 1:20 (NIV)

God, I am happy that the promises in your word pertain to me. Your goodness is guaranteed because I am in Christ. I declare that it is not a matter of if you will fulfill your promises but when.

Today, paint your promises on my heart so that I may have them with me at all times. I decree and declare that confessing "amen" brings your promises to life. Amen comes after a prayer because it means "so be it." It is my faith statement to give the glory back to you.

Thank you for saying yes.

In Jesus' name, I pray. Amen.

Show Me How

Give to everyone what you owe them: Pay your taxes and government fees to those who collect them, and give respect and honor to those who are in authority.
Romans 13:7 (NLT)

God, it is hard to respect authority when you feel like authority does not respect you. However, I know I must give respect to get it. Right now, society has shown me different as providing respect does not guarantee it will be reciprocated. God, give me your view on this situation. Help me to act in the same way you would.

I believe in my heart that you would respect all people. Help me to do the same as I know in doing so I am ultimately showing my respect for you. God, help me to use my brain to create change in the way that you would. Teach me how to seek justice and correct oppression. I pray for invaluable insight to make this world better. Help me to keep fighting for what is right even when it is hard to push through what is happening right now. I know that in due season a harvest is going to come.

I declare that better leadership and authority figures are coming. Systems are changing to reflect true justice and equality. I believe that you are raising up people to improve the current operations of the world. God, I want to help, show me how.

In Jesus' name, I pray. Amen.

People Pleaser

And when he had sent the multitudes away, he went up into a mountain apart to pray: and when the evening was come, he was there alone.
Matthew 14:23 (KJV)

Dear God, sometimes I have a fear of missing out. I want to be at everything and go everywhere. God, I have not spent much alone time with you. Help me to reprioritize. Help me to stop living in response to people, more than I live in response to you.

God, I pray that you help me to stop being a people pleaser. I desire to be satisfied with you. You are the everlasting God and King of my life. The whole earth will be filled with your glory. You are doing exceedingly more than I could have ever thought to ask. You have established me according to the gospel of Jesus Christ. You are more than deserving of my time.

Today, I will make time to spend privately with you.

In Jesus' name, I pray. Amen.

Don't Stop Forgiving

Even if they sin against you seven times in a day and seven times come back to you saying, 'I repent,' you must forgive them."
Luke 17:4 (NIV)

God, I have been working on showing forgiveness. Now, I am being tested. The same person keeps doing me wrong, and I think it is intentional. How do you forgive a person like this sincerely?

God, show me the way. You have forgiven me thousands of times for committing the same sin. I see just how much love it took for you to do that. God, drive out the hate in my heart with your love. Help me to look past the people who continuously hurt me. Help me to take the opportunity to pray for them.

Hurt people, hurt people and I pray healing for them right now. I pray that you strengthen them to let go of their bad habits. God, grab hold of their situation and help them to be better. God, forgive them for they know not what they do.

In Jesus' name, I pray. Amen.

Felt It

For we have not a high priest which cannot be touched with the feeling of our infirmities; but was in all points tempted like as we are, yet without sin.
Hebrews 4:15 (KJV)

God, you are marvelous. My reality does not supersede your ability to understand what I go through. You know exactly what I feel because you felt it. You felt my pain from rejection and my sorrow from death. Thank you for taking walks in my shoes.

God, give me your willpower to stand the test of time. Remind me that I am never alone when I feel I am. Help me to see that you are in this with me no matter how it seems. No sadness, fear, grief, anger, or shame can separate me from you – because you felt it too.

Help me to recover in the same way you did. You did not allow anything or circumstance to define or defeat you. Help me, God.

In Jesus' name, I pray. Amen.

Just Say It

Whenever you are arrested and brought to trial, do not worry beforehand about what to say. Just say whatever is given you at the time, for it is not you speaking, but the Holy Spirit.
Mark 13:11 (NIV)

God, I come to you today thanking you for speaking to me. I pray that you allow me to hear and apply what you say. Sometimes you tell me to say things that I do not quite understand, but I pray for the boldness to say it anyway. I pray for the courage to speak the truth. I pray for gentleness when I have to deliver bad news.

Help me to stop worrying about having specific conversations. When I am confronted or must face a challenging situation, I pray that you speak for me. I declare that the words I say will be edifying in all cases. God, your word declares that I can have whatever I say, so if I say what you say, I know I will be okay.

In Jesus' name, I pray. Amen.

Recommendation Denied

The thoughts of the righteous are right: but the counsels of the wicked are deceit.
Proverbs 12:5 (KJV)

You are a God of order. You are a God of keen instruction. You are also a God who gives me a choice to do what I want. Often people tell me what they think I should do. They say what they think they see in me. They tell me what they believe you told them about me. God forgive me for allowing just anyone to speak things over my life.

My prayer today is that you help me to use your sense to deny anything spoken to me that you did not order. People's advice does not trump your truth. I declare that their opinions will not fade out my faith. God, remove the thoughts that I took on from others that were not from you. Give me the discernment to know when to accept and when to deny advice.

In Jesus' name, I pray. Amen.

I Feel Good

This is the day the Lord has made. We will rejoice and be glad in it.
Psalm 118:24 (NLT)

Today, I feel good! I am blessed and destined for this day. God, nothing can stop me today because this is the day that you have made. I will hold on to my hope no matter what happens today. I declare that faith will help me find my way throughout today. I will be grateful because your grace is with me.

A lot of people did not live to see this day, but you chose to allow me too. I will rejoice and be glad.

In Jesus' name, I pray. Amen.

I Figured It Out

If you need wisdom, ask our generous God, and he will give it to you. He will not rebuke you for asking.
James 1:5 (NLT)

God, thank you for revealing things to me I would have otherwise never known. Thank you for giving me the intelligence to figure things out. I figured out how prayer works. I figured out how to please you with my life. I figured out how to tap into your spiritual realm.

Now that I have trust, things that were once difficult are now easy. Now that I comprehend your word, weights I use to carry I do not carry anymore. Now that I confess you as Lord of my life, my ticket into heaven is punched in.

I once lacked wisdom but I asked for it and you gave it to me. My fear of you has given me knowledge. Wisdom has protected me. Thank You.

In Jesus' name, I pray. Amen.

Yes, I Can

Now someone may argue, "Some people have faith; others have good deeds." But I say, "How can you show me your faith if you don't have good deeds? I will show you my faith by my good deeds."
James 2:18 (NLT)

God, remind me that I have what it takes. You said that I am an extension of you. I have never seen you not accomplish something you set out to achieve. You call me your workmanship created for good works. Remove all the fear and doubt that exist within me. I declare that I will live to declare the works of the Lord. I am confident that you will complete the good work you started in me. Thank you for giving me what it takes to beat all odds.

In Jesus' name, I pray. Amen.

Think Then Speak

So, encourage each other and build each other up, just as you are already doing.
1 Thessalonians 5:11 (NLT)

God, forgive me if I hurt someone with my words. Sometimes I underestimate how my words can affect other people. Help me to be more watchful of the things I say and the way I speak them. Correct my intentions to match the impact that I want to have. Search my heart and seal my lips when things that are not edifying try to come out.

God, I pray that you help me to control my gut reactions and immediate responses. Forgive me for letting corrupt talk come out of my mouth. Help me to think before I speak. Help me to show hospitality. I pray that you help me to speak positive things that can give hope to those that hear.

In Jesus' name, I pray. Amen.

No More Hypocrite in Me

*When you make a promise to God, don't delay in
following through, for God takes no pleasure in fools.
Keep all the promises you make to him.*
Ecclesiastes 5:4 (NLT)

God, forgive me for breaking my promises. I promised that if
you got me out the last situation I would not go back and I
did. I have lied, pretending to live in complete submission to
you. Forgive me for being a hypocrite. Forgive me for not
keeping my promises. Forgive me for making promises on a
stipulation of your power. Forgive me for trying to pitch my
promises to you in exchange for grace, mercy, and favor.

God, I pray that you would have mercy on me! This time I
am going to follow through with my promises. I am going to
live in reverence of your name. Forgive me for insulting your
intelligence. I declare that I will keep the promises I make to
you.

In Jesus' name, I pray. Amen.

Closer

And the child grew and became strong in spirit; and he lived in the wilderness until he appeared publicly to Israel.
Luke 1:80 (NIV)

God in heaven hallowed be your name. I thank you for taking me through the storms to reveal my strength. I thank you for every test and trial that made me who I am today. I appreciate every disappointment that showed me your ways are better than mine. God, I decree that my biggest breakthrough is closer than I think.

God, debut my destiny in the next 30 days. Give me the strength to go through the rain I prayed for you to send. Trouble is going to get thicker than ever, but your grace will abound. If pain tries to wreck my body, cast it back to the pits of hell from which it came. I decree and declare I will not be defeated, I will be closer.

I believe that victory is coming by day 10! Biblically 10 represents a testimony. I decree that in 10 days I will have a testimony of your power, of your grace, and unmerited favor. Although you slay me, I will I trust you.

In Jesus' name, I pray. Amen.

Fixed Mindset

Set your minds on things above, not on earthly things.
Colossians 3:2 (NIV)

God, I trust you. I believe that you predestine my purpose and potential. There is no cap on the glory and grace you extend to me. You are the same God today, yesterday, and forever more. Today, I am going to stick with what things I know are for certain.

I know that if I keep my eyes focused on you, I cannot sink in the sorrows of this world. I know that if I look to the hills, my help will come. I know that in moments of frustration you will keep me in perfect peace. I know that if I lean not on my own understanding, you will direct my path. I know that prayer, fasting, tithing, and being obedient works.

God, help me to have a fixed mindset when it comes to your power and promises. I pray that you help me to see that in you somethings never change. Help me to understand that if I fix my mind on the things written in your word, I will be just fine.

In Jesus' name, I pray. Amen.

No Strings Attached

If you lend money to one of my people among you who is
needy, do not treat it like a business deal; charge no
interest.
Exodus 22:25 (NIV)

God, thank you for not charging me extra for your blessings. I
pray that you help me to bless others in the same way you
bless me. Help me to give without expecting extra in return.
God, help me to do things out of the kindness of my heart.
God, I pray that you deal with those who take advantage of
that. Free me from worrying about who owes me. Instead, I
pray blessings over them who need to borrow.

Thank you for the putting people in my life who gave to me
when I needed it. I pray that you to continue to bless them.
Today, I pray that you make me a lender and not a borrower.
Make me the head and not the tail. Prosper everything that I
touch.

In Jesus' name, I pray. Amen.

Side Piece

Woe to the world because of the things that cause people to stumble! Such things must come, but woe to the person through whom they come!
Matthew 18:7 (NIV)

God, thank you for creating marriage. I pray that my marriage is held in high honor among all. God, I come against the spirit that dwells amongst men and women who justify their role as a "side piece." I pray that you have mercy on their souls for they know not what they do. Forgive them, God. You are not mocked, and they will reap what they sow.

God, help them to fill their voids with you. Help them to find satisfaction in the word, not in another person's spouse. God, I pray that you saturate their minds with good sense. Destroy every yoke and desire of theirs that longs for another person's spouse. God, free them from the bondage in their beliefs and the manipulation in their minds.

I pray restoration for every broken family. I pray healing over every hurt heart. I declare that my marriage will be covered in your blood.

In Jesus' name, I pray. Amen.

Who's Your Daddy?

Yours, Lord, is the greatness and the power and the glory and the majesty and the splendor, for everything in heaven and earth is yours. Yours, Lord, is the kingdom; you are exalted as head over all.
1 Chronicles 29:11 (NIV)

God, you are Alpha and Omega! You are the beginning and the end. You hold all power in your hands. You are seated on the throne in majesty. The world was created by the words that you spoke. Everything that we see and the things we cannot see are possible because of you.

You are mighty, God and it is in you that I have my being. You come to my defense and fight for me. You are rich in mercy! You have raised me up and seated me in heavenly places with you.

You are my father, and you are a good one - in you will I trust.

In Jesus' name, I pray. Amen.

Good People, Bad Things

*Blessed is the one who perseveres under trial because,
having stood the test, that person will receive the crown of
life that the Lord has promised to those who love him.*
James 1:12 (NIV)

I can make it through anything with your help. I am a good person, and you are a good God. Bad things happened to you therefore it is no surprise that you would allow some bad things to happen to me. Even though you slay me, I will trust you! I will not lose heart. In your silence, I will trust your presence is near.

I will stand the test to be blessed. I believe that no matter what you bring me to, you will see me through. You are training me for war. You are teaching me to become more dependent on you. You have me in this season to remind me that it is better to trust in you than in man.

I will rejoice in our shared sufferings.

In Jesus' name, I pray. Amen.

Built to Last

Let your roots grow down into him, and let your lives be built on him. Then your faith will grow strong in the truth you were taught, and you will overflow with thankfulness.
Colossians 2:7 (NLT)

God, thank you for making me strong. Thank you for assembling me with all your best parts. You are the mechanic of my life. Thank you for fixing what broke. You have fixed my focus, replaced my weaknesses, and tuned up my trust. I pray that you make your word my windshield. God, gas me up with your grace. Help me to maintain the blessing you have built me to be.

In Jesus' name, I pray. Amen.

Influence My Influencers

The fear of the Lord is the beginning of wisdom: a good understanding have all they that do his commandments: his praise endureth for ever.
Psalm 111:10 (KJV)

God, some people in my life have strong influences on me. They influence my thoughts and actions. I look up to them, and I value their input.

God, help them as they help me. Be their biggest influence. Lead them and speak to them. I pray that you strengthen their faith, increase their income, and provide for them. God be the peace in their homes and unity in their families. I pray that you draw them closer to you. Give them a thirst for righteousness.

God, I pray that no weapon formed against them shall prosper. Make them the head, not the tail. I declare that they will lend and not borrow. I pray that everything they touch thrives and brings glory to your name. I pray that you bless them with the desires of their hearts.

In Jesus' name, I pray. Amen.

Pure Gold

But he knows the way that I take; when he has tested me, I will come forth as gold.
Job 23:10 (NIV)

God, no matter what you take me through I will come out as pure gold. I will endure whatever test I will have just to see your name be praised. I will stop whining and get the word to find my strength. I decree double for my trouble!

God, you are the assessor of my wealth. Make this trouble worth it. The devil's plan may seem to be working. It may even get me down, but I thank you for being a God who will pick me up.

In Jesus' name, I pray. Amen.

Stop Being Mean

Do not fret because of those who are evil or be envious of those who do wrong; for like the grass they will soon wither, like green plants they will soon die away.
Psalm 37:1-2 (NIV)

God, you are one of a kind. I come before you today to thank you for your goodness. I pray for a gentle spirit like yours. I thank you for never being mean to me but always being mindful of an opportunity to show me how to be better.

God forgive me for being mean to people and forgive those who are mean to me. God, I give my mean-spirited ways over to you today. Forgive me for wanting to hurt people just because they hurt me. Forgive me for justifying my actions when I know they are wrong. Show me a better way to discipline, communicate, and interact with others.

I repent for hurting people who did not do anything to me. Please forgive me and make me better.

In Jesus' name, I pray. Amen.

Do Right

The LORD is good to all; he has compassion on all he has made.
Psalm 145:9 (NIV)

God, you are holy, and you are wonderful. You are worthy of all my praise and honor. You are matchless, and I thank you for keeping no record of my wrongdoings. I thank you for not having a do right or get left mentality. You have been here with me through every right turn and every wrong one too.

Today, I thank you for blessing me with another opportunity to get things right. I make a vow to do things right because tomorrow is not promised. At any moment you can come back, and I do not want to be left here when you do.

God, show me what to do so that I do not get left behind. Reveal to me what areas I need to improve on.

In Jesus' name, I pray. Amen.

Just God

*He rules the world in righteousness and judges the peoples
with equity.*
Psalm 9:8 (NIV)

God, thank you for blessing me right now! I thank you for
protecting me right now from the things that may have killed
me later. I thank you for taking things away that I was
holding on to out of comfort. Thank you for removing the
blinders from my eyes and showing me the true colors of
those I called friends. God, I thank you for judging all
situations in fairness. Things did not seem fair then, but I
know that it was you working in equity and love. Thank you
for being a just God.

In Jesus' name, I pray. Amen.

Mornings & Mercy

Have you ever commanded the morning to appear and caused the dawn to rise in the east? Have you made daylight spread to the ends of the earth, to bring an end to the night's wickedness?
Job 38:12-13 (NLT)

God, thank you for waking me up this morning and starting me on my way. I pray that mornings bring newness to my life. I pray for new joy, fresh favor, and miracles every day. I will seek you first in the morning and watch all things work in my favor during the day. God rid me of the troubles of yesterday, today.

I decree and declare that mornings do not just begin when the before noon. I pray that mornings be when the "son" rises. God, Jesus is your son, and he has already risen. I decree and declare that every time I call on the name of Jesus morning will come. Every time I call on the name of Jesus' darkness will fade away.

In Jesus' name, I pray. Amen.

Hold on Me

Teaching them to observe all things whatsoever I have commanded you: and, lo, I am with you always, even unto the end of the world. Amen.
Matthew 28:20 (KJV)

God, thank you for having a firm hold on me, even when I tried to leave your love glued me to grace. Thank you for sticking your Spirit on my soul. Your convicting Spirit steered me back to you whenever I was doing wrong. You have a hold on me! A tight grip that no devil in hell can loosen. Today, I declare victory over Satan. No matter how far I venture off on the side of sin, sin cannot win. You are going to come after me and fight for me.

In Jesus' name, I pray. Amen.

Tricks

Praise God, who did not ignore my prayer or withdraw his unfailing love from me.
Psalm 66:20 (NLT)

Today my mind will stop playing tricks on me. Just because someone very close to me died does not mean I must die with them. God help me to see that you are still in this with me. The enemy cannot trick my mind. He cannot make me believe that I am next. I will not allow the enemy to trick my mind under no circumstances.

The devil wants me to believe that you do not want to talk to me because there have been times I did not want to talk to you. I know that you still hear me when I pray. I know that you still see me, and you still care.

The devil prowls around looking to devour me, but God hide me in your secret place. Please do not let me be led astray.

In Jesus' name, I pray. Amen.

Take the Credit

Thou art worthy, O Lord, to receive glory and honour and
power: for thou hast created all things, and for thy
pleasure they are and were created.
Revelation 4:11 (KJV)

No one can stop me because you want to see me win. It is for
this that all credit belongs to you. You are the creator of all
things. Thank you for blessing me with insight, skill, and
creativity to use things for my pleasure.

I have never accomplished anything without you. Forgive me
for ever thinking I did. It is no question of who should take
the credit for my life. God, all the glory belongs to you for all
the marvelous things you have done. For all the doors you
opened, closed, and propped open – I praise you.

In Jesus' name, I pray. Amen.

24 Hours

From the rising of the sun unto the going down of the same
the Lord's name is to be praised.
Psalm 113:3 (KJV)

God, thank you for waking me up today and starting me on
my way! I thank you for the activity of my limbs and
allowing me to see a brand-new day! For the next 24 hours,
help me to put my attention on you. Help me to dwell in your
presence like never before.

Right now, I claim that the next 24 hours will be hours of
stillness. Release me from the cares of this world so that I can
spend uninterrupted time with you. As I go through my day,
help me to find your peace. God, help me to hear your voice.
Speak to me and tell me what you want me to know.

Show me how to make the most of my days. With all, I have
going on days seem to fly faster than planes. Show me how to
find stillness in your presence every day.

In Jesus' name, I pray. Amen.

The Switch Up

But many who are the greatest now will be least important then, and those who seem least important now will be the greatest then.
Mark 10:30 (NLT)

Dear Heavenly Father, I come to you because I believe that things are not what they seem. I may feel inadequate now, but I know a change is coming. Things that I share with people may go in one ear and out another, but I decree that a shift is on its way.

God, I believe that you are going to elevate me in this season. I believe that you are going to give me a new language, vocabulary, and speech to reach a whole new audience. An audience where the market is not over saturated but needs to be saturated by your spirit. You are going to recommend me for new opportunities designed just for me.

God, compliment me with the confidence and courage I need to operate in my greatness. Put together a purpose pack of believers who will pray me through this journey. I decree that I am not only amongst the great but that I am also great.

In Jesus' name, I pray. Amen.

From Dark to Light

*The Lord is my light and my salvation – so why should I
be afraid? The Lord is my fortress, protecting me from
danger, so why should I tremble?*
Psalm 27:1 (NLT)

God, thank you for being my light. You are with me even
when my days seem dark. You are my present help at the
time of trouble. Help me not to be afraid of the terror at night
or the arrows that fly by day. Help me to not be afraid when
things do not turn out the way I hoped.

Today, I declare that I can see. I am no longer blinded my
problems. I thank you, that fear did not stop me from putting
my hope in you. When the night comes, I will think of the
goodness you showed me throughout the day. I rebuke the
spirit of restlessness that may try to keep me up at night. God
make my gloom glorious as you said you would do in Isaiah
9:1.

I decree that I am a chosen to be an overcomer. I will
proclaim you as excellent for you are the God that called me
out of the darkness. Thank you for being my fortress. You are
all the protection I could ever need.

In Jesus' name, I pray. Amen.

Time Out

Send me a sign of your favor. Then those who hate me will be put to shame, for you, O Lord, help and comfort me.
Psalm 86:17 (NLT)

God, I know that you have my back. Today, I pray that you silence the naysayers. Send your power to be my army in this war. Help me to see that not everyone will like me because not everyone liked you. I know that some people will only hate me because the favor they thought they had, rests on me instead. God, I will not fret or concern myself with things that do not bring you glory.

I believe that things are being worked out. God, put the haters in time out and block out their ability to have any influence on me. God, I do not doubt your power. I do not doubt that your favor is upon me. Favor is bestowed upon me because I walk uprightly. Thank you for your lifetime supply of favor. I pray that it follows me all the days of my life.

In Jesus' name, I pray. Amen.

Exercise Wisdom

If you need wisdom, ask our generous God, and he will
give it to you. He will not rebuke you for asking.
James 1:5 (NLT)

God, help me to exercise wisdom daily. Help me to use
wisdom in all of the decisions I make. Order my steps in the
way that I should go. God, I cry out to you for help. I ask that
you help me in the areas I am confused on what to do. God,
remove all timid tendencies that I feel when I come to you in
prayer.

You told me to come boldly to the throne of grace so that I
may find help in my time of need. God bless me with your
keen wisdom from above. I pray for irrefutable wisdom so no
man can deny. God, make me wise beyond my years. Give
me your knowledge and help me to understand how to use it
for your glory in the best way possible.

In Jesus' name, I pray. Amen.

Demons Are Not Dumb

You believe that there is one God. Good! Even the demons believe that – and shudder.
James 2:19 (NIV)

God, you are the only true and living God. Every devil in hell knows this to be true. They also know that faith without works is dead which is why they try to stop me from doing the things I know I should. God, strengthen me against my hell bound opponents. Help me to know their every move so that I can fight my way to safety.

Today, I shout Jesus over every circumstance in my life. I declare Jesus over my energy today. I proclaim Jesus as Lord over my life. I decree that the power in the name of Jesus' will stop the devil's plan. I decree and declare that every demon that tries to invade my space will submit to me in Jesus' name.

God, do not let the devil outsmart me for he knows your word too. I decree and declare that no weapon that is formed against me shall prosper.

In Jesus' name, I pray. Amen.

Remember the Rescue

My child, never forget the things I have taught you. Store
my commands in your heart.
Proverbs 3:1 (NLT)

God, thank you for teaching me lesson's I never knew I
needed to learn. I am grateful for the tough moments in my
life that helped to craft my character. The lessons I learned
cost others their lives, goals, and dreams. I am so glad that
the situations I experienced did not cause me to lose my life.

God, as I read your word, I pray that you allow it to marinate
in my mind. Help me never to forget the lessons you have
taught me through my trials and tribulations. God, make my
heart your journal. Store your commandments and promises
in it so I will never lose sight of them.

In Jesus' name, I pray. Amen.

Answer Me

Ask me and I will tell you remarkable secrets you do not know about things to come.
Jeremiah 33:3 (NLT)

God, am I operating in your will? You said that if I called on you, you would answer me. Tell me what you want me to know. Show me where you want me to go. I am in need of answers to my prayer requests.

God, I know you hear me. Give me the strength to wait for your answers. I am not praying for things to be easier but for the path to be more evident so I can know what to do. God, you said that if I ask anything according to your will, you will hear me. I am asking for direction.

God, you know my heart, and I ask that you search my motives. Correct them if they are wrong. God, give me the spiritual ears to hear your voice.

In Jesus' name, I pray. Amen.

Fellowship

*And let us not neglect our meeting together, as some people
do, but encourage one another, especially now that the day
of his return is drawing near.*
Hebrews 10:25 (NLT)

God, I believe that you created fellowship because it is
essential in helping me build my relationship with you. I pray
that you bring people into my life who has similar spiritual
goals as me. God, I pray that you send authentic people who
are not judgmental.

God, place me in the right places so that I can find other
believers to network with. Remove the cautiousness from me
I sometimes feel when you are the topic of conversation. Give
me a new level of boldness to share my experience in hopes
to encourage someone else.

God, I believe that you are coming back soon. I do not know
when, but I know I want to go back with you when you do. I
am praying that you send people into my life who can help
encourage me until that day comes. The devil is really on his
job as he is trying to turn people away from you. I pray that
you keep me from falling into the trap. Keep me grounded in
the truth.

In Jesus' name, I pray. Amen.

No Signs

When you go through deep waters, I will be with you.
When you go through rivers of difficulty, you will not
drown. When you walk through the fire of oppression, you
will not be burned up; the flames will not consume you.
Isaiah 43:2 (NLT)

God, I can recall multiple times when I was in a bind, and you helped me out. I can remember when I felt like I was sinking, but my faith made me float. Thank you for keeping me safe. I appreciate you for looking out for me even when I was not looking out for myself. God, you protected me through the thick and thin. Your mercy hid my name and removed all the signs from my past.

Thank you for making me look better than where I came from. I made it because you pulled me through. Without you, there would be no me. God, I thank you for all the things you have done. Thank you for separating my past from my future.

In Jesus' name, I pray. Amen.

Value Over Vanity

For by the grace given me I say to every one of you: Do not think of yourself more highly than you ought, but rather think of yourself with sober judgment, in accordance with the faith God has distributed to each of you.
Romans 12:3 (NIV)

Dear God, you made me just as I am. You placed the value on my life before I was conceived in my mother's womb. Nothing that I do can ever change the value you have already placed on me. God, forgive me for the times I was vain and self-centered. I pray that you deliver me from my prideful nature which can make me think more highly of myself than I ought to.

Show me how to be proud of my progress and successes without being boastful. I repent for thinking that I am better than others.

In Jesus' name, I pray. Amen.

A Life of Loyalty

In the same way, those of you who do not give up
everything you have cannot be my disciples.
Luke 14:33 (NIV)

My Father in heaven, thank you for being loyal to me. I pray that you help me to live a life of loyalty. So many people pride themselves on loyalty but neglect to be loyal to you. God, make me better. I pray that my loyalty is to you first and foremost.

God, help me to be loyal to you even if it means I am disloyal to someone else. I decree that people will not take your place in my life. God, you are my life. I owe it all to you. Teach me why loyalty is an essential part of our relationship. I pray that you ingrain in me the attitude, wisdom, and knowledge needed to live in complete submission to you as a loyal believer.

In Jesus' name, I pray. Amen.

The Redemption

In whom we have redemption through his blood, the
forgiveness of sins, according to the riches of his grace.
Ephesians 1:7 (KJV)

Jesus, your blood will not go wasted! I confess that I am a sinner and I ask for your forgiveness. I will no longer hold on to my sins in shame. You died that I may have life and it more abundantly. You took the nails in your hands and feet so that I could have the right to be forgiven. You were beaten so that sickness would not beat me. You died on the cross so that I did not have to carry the weight of my sins.

Help me to remember that your grace covers every one of my faults. I pray that you free me from misinterpreted beliefs that make me think I cannot talk to you as a sinner. I believe that care about me even in my sin. God, teach me how to accept your redeeming power.

In Jesus' name, I pray. Amen.

Help Me Believe

Jesus said unto him, if thou canst believe, all things are possible to him that believeth.
Mark 9:23 (KJV)

God, help me to understand why bad things happen to innocent people. God, I know that your word says you want what is best for me, but I pray that you help me to believe this. You crafted me in excellence and with purposed precision. I pray that you help me to see that the bad things that have happened to me were not my fault.

The times when I felt abandoned, misused, and abused were not a result of something I did. God, I pray that you remove any trauma from my memory. Allow your love to fill every void that exists in my life. Even when I do not feel like it, I will decree and declare it because it was not my fault!

God, thank you for releasing me from self-blame. Thank you for changing the trajectory of my life. Thank you for canceling my past so it could not subscribe to my future.

In Jesus' name, I pray. Amen.

Get Up

*And God hath both raised up the Lord, and will also raise
up us by his own power.*
1 Corinthians 6:14 (KJV)

God, thank you for extending your power to me. Since Jesus
got up from the grave, I know I can get up and start again! I
know that there is nothing too hard to bounce back from.

Disappointments, shame, sin, or guilt will never be enough to
keep me bound. You reminded me multiple times that when
it seems all hope is lost, you are here.

I declare Acts 2:24 over me today which says, "But God
released him from the horrors of death and raised him back
to life, for death could not keep him in its grip." God, this
scripture lets me know that you hold all power. It reminds
me that prayer still works. It reassures me that no one
compares to you! I will take pleasure in knowing that nothing
can hold me down when you are around.

In Jesus' name, I pray. Amen.

Help Me, Love Me

*After all, no one ever hated their own body, but they feed
and care for their body, just as Christ does the church.*
Ephesians 5:29 (NIV)

God, I pray that you help me to respect myself more. I bind
the spirit low self-esteem and depression that tries to make
me question my existence and worth. God, I put your
presence in my room. I pray that you cover my eyes with
your adoration of me so that all I see when I look in the
mirror is a reflection of you.

I decree that I will love who I am. I declare that I will cherish
myself the same way that you love the church. Help me to
find my self-assurance in you. God forgive me for trying to
change myself to match the uniqueness of others. Today, I
will see myself the way that you see me.

In Jesus' name, I pray. Amen.

Overthinking

I can do nothing on my own. I judge as God tells me.
Therefore, my judgment is just, because I carry out the will
of the one who sent me, not my own will.
John 5:30 (NLT)

Jesus, help me to simplify my life. I pray that you help me to stop overthinking everything that requires my input. My input does not matter if it does not have your output.

Help me to hear you better as you speak. Keep me from being lost in my train of thought. God, I pray that you write your will in my mind so that my steps can be ordered by you. Remove me out of my own way so that your glory can be made known to others.

In Jesus' name, I pray. Amen.

Grow Up

As newborn babes, desire the sincere milk of the word, that ye may grow thereby.
1 Peter 2:2 (KJV)

God, I cannot grow without you. I am craving for more of your spirit. I need you to fill me with the nutrients from your word. I need you to sustain me with your Spirit.

God, ignite in me a never-ending desire to have you. For your word says in Hebrews 5:14, that "solid food is for those who are mature, who through training have the skill to recognize the difference between right and wrong." God, I pray that you prepare me to function as an adult in Christ. God, give me a mature appetite for your word.

In Jesus' name, I pray. Amen.

Relax

Being confident of this, that he who began a good work in you will carry it on to completion until the day of Christ Jesus.
Philippians 1:6 (NIV)

God, it looks like time is running out, but I know that you are in control. Today, I pray that you help me to relax. No matter at what point I started, I know you are going to see me through. Take my goals and deadlines in exchange for your will. God, I have faith in you. I know you will complete the good work you ordered in me. Help me to remember that what you order you will pay for, you will never leave a tap unpaid. I may not have all the finances to carry out the vision, but you do.

I pray for peace and freedom from anxiousness.

In Jesus' name, I pray. Amen.

Let It Go

I, even I, am he who blots out your transgressions, for my own sake, and remembers your sins no more.
Isaiah 43:25 (NIV)

God, some things you have forgiven me for I still hold on too. Help me to stop keeping a record of my sins. Sometimes I put myself through turmoil by replaying regret.

God, help me to live in the freedom that you give. I come against the spirit of confusion that wants to kill my joy. You forgive me. Help me to forgive myself. I bind the spirit of regret that wants to rid me of peace. God, you forgive me, please help me to do the same. God, no matter how many mistakes I make you love me just the same.

Remove any teaching or message from my memory that contradicts this.

In Jesus' name, I pray. Amen.

Stubborn Stabs

Whoever stubbornly refuses to accept criticism will suddenly be destroyed beyond recovery.
Proverbs 29:1 (NLT)

God deliver me from being stubborn. I admit that I have my moments. I do not want to be destroyed because I am too stubborn to listen. I do not want my blessings cut short because I cut people off for correcting me when I was wrong.

God, I thank you for placing brave individuals in my life who are not afraid to tell me when I am wrong. I pray that you bless them for trying to help me. God, forgive me if I ever offended someone who attempted to give me criticism I needed to hear. God, I need to be corrected when I am wrong. I pray that you help me to stop feeling attacked. Help me to stop feeling so powerful and perfect because I am neither.

Remove the wounds that stubbornness has caused in my life. I decree that I will be open to criticism today. I will not take everything someone says to heart. God, you hold my heart, and I pray you continue to protect it.

In Jesus' name, I pray. Amen.

Second Chance

Yet I still dare to hope when I remember this: The faithful love of the Lord never ends! His mercies never cease.
Lamentations 3:21 (NLT)

God forgive me for blocking things from my life you created me to have. You created me to have love and peace, and I accept it now. I take your abundance of mercy and grace. God, I accept the second chance you have given me by waking me up today.

Life has not always been easy. Things you promised me came at a cost, and it was not always pleasant. Forgive me for trying to protect myself when you are the protector. I should have never tried to fill your shoes in my life. God, I repent for overstepping my boundaries. I am sorry for not completely trusting you as my Lord.

Today, I pray that you open me back up to receive the things I closed myself off from. Restore me, God. Restore health, wealth, and release the things that were held up because of my unbelief.

In Jesus' name, I pray. Amen.

Strength Take Over

*He will wipe every tear from their eyes, and there will be
no more death or sorrow or crying or pain. All these things
are gone forever.*
Revelation 21:4 (NLT)

God, sometimes I feel like my strength is leaving. I come to
you asking you to help me make it through. I cannot see my
way, but I know you are in the midst. God, I am praying for
an outpour of your might and strength.

I pray that strength takes over me today for I am getting
tired. God, touch me so that I can be made whole again.
God, replace my weaknesses with yours. For you said in 1
Corinthians 1:25, that even your weakness is greater than my
strength. God, wipe away every worry. Make my strong days
consistent.

In Jesus' name, I pray. Amen.

The Gifts

Now to each one the manifestation of the Spirit is given for the common good.
1 Corinthians 12:7 (NIV)

I have extraordinary gifts, and I will use them to bring your name glory! God, thank you for not leaving me out when you decided to bless people today with talents and abilities. I know that I have an assignment to use the gifts you gave to me. God, I pray that you enlighten me with wisdom, clear understanding, and vision to walk in the purpose of my gifts.

I pray that these gifts be used to spread life and encouragement to those who lack it. God, allow my gifts to be beneficial for all who need them. I pray that you give me the confidence to fully utilize my gifts. Forgive me for trying to substitute my gifts for other ones that seemed more appealing. I believe that you gave me these specifics talents, abilities, and gifts because I am qualified to operate in them.

In Jesus' name, I pray. Amen.

I Have a Choice

And said, Verily I say unto you, except ye be converted,
and become as little children, ye shall not enter into the
kingdom of heaven.
Matthew 18:3 (KJV)

My prayer today is that you help me to find my innocence again. God, make me blameless in your sight so that I can make it to heaven. Give me a fresh start Jesus. Forgive me for the sins I have committed against you. Your word says in 1 John 1:9, "if I confess my sins, you would forgive me and cleanse me from unrighteousness."

I want another opportunity to show you I can be who you called me to be. Thank you for not counting me out even when others did. I know that my choices will either lead me to heaven or send me to hell. God, I choose heaven. Help me to live according to the choice I have made.

In Jesus' name, I pray. Amen.

Use My Mistakes

*He that covereth his sins shall not prosper: but whoso
confesseth and forsaketh them shall have mercy.*
Proverbs 28:13 (KJV)

God, forgive me for I have sinned and fallen short of your
glory. Today, I expose my sins to you. Use my mistakes to
spread a message that you are merciful and just to forgive.
You have redeeming power!

Use my mistakes to spread a message of freedom. I am not
burdened down, broken, or defeated anymore. I pray for the
ones who still are, God, send a signal of love to them today.
Help them to see that you are the supplier of freedom.

I would never have asked you to use my mistakes, but I
realized that you used someone else's to teach me and they
brought me to you. I cannot conceal your grace and mercy
towards me. Help me to open up and be real about how you
have saved my soul.

In Jesus' name, I pray. Amen.

Spirit Led

But the natural man receiveth not the things of the Spirit of God: for they are foolishness unto him: neither can he know them, because they are spiritually discerned.
1 Corinthians 2:14 (KJV)

Father God, I come to you because I am in need of your Spirit. I come seeking to attain what man alone cannot. I come seeking your presence that I might reach the wisdom that is only available for those who are connected to your Spirit.

I decree and declare that I shall walk in the counsel of your Spirit. God, renew and awaken my mind with your Spirit. I pray that you quicken my mind with your Spirit. I declare that I will operate in "God-speed." I pray that you elevate me in every area of my life with your Spirit.

Father God I thank you in advance for your Spirit. Reveal your will to me that I might walk upright as a child of God.

In Jesus' name, I pray. Amen.

1 Am Qualified

But God hath chosen the foolish things of the world to confound the wise; and God hath chosen the weak things of the world to confound the things which are mighty.
1 Corinthians 1:27 (KJV)

Father God, I want to thank you for creating me and stamping me with your approval. I come to you with thanksgiving on my lips as I pray for new opportunities in life. I pray that you give me innovative thoughts to create and sustain new things in the earth.

I come knowing that in man eye's I might not have the proper credentials to obtain the things that I desire. However, I come to pronounce in your presence that I am qualified. I decree that every door that is off limits to me be made available because of your favor. I decree that every area of lack in my life be filled with your wisdom. In every area of weakness, God, plug in your strength that I might exceed the expectation of man.

I will be who you say I am and do what you say I can do.

In Jesus' name, I pray. Amen.

Setbacks Set Me Up

For a just man falleth seven times, and riseth up again: but the wicked shall fall into mischief.
Proverbs 24:16 (KJV)

Father God, I come to you because you are God. I know that all things are possible for those who believe in you. Life has taken me through many of mountain tops and valleys. As I face another difficult time in life, I ask that you give me the strength to overcome as you have done many times before. I declare that I am an overcomer. I am victorious. I declare that all setbacks are setting me up for greater.

God, you formed me, so I know that you will fill me. Everything that was taken from me was only you making room for what is next to come. I expect the best, so I shall receive it.

In Jesus' name, I pray. Amen.

Blocked Blessings

If ye be willing and obedient, ye shall eat the good of the land.
Isaiah 1:19 (KJV)

God, test my willingness and obedience. I pray that you help me to listen. Help me to hear your voice through the crowd of opinions. Clear out chaotic confusion so that I do not miss what you are saying to me. God, my spirit is willing, yet my flesh is weak. I pray that you help me to be obedient so that my disobedience does not block me from your blessings.

God, I desire to live in obedience to your word. Block anything that tries to lead me astray from your instructions. Free me from my stubbornness, ignorance, and pride. I surrender to you God. I pray that you have your way in my life.

In Jesus' name, I pray. Amen.

Rejected Not Subjected

The righteous cry out, and the Lord hears them; he delivers them from all their troubles. The Lord is close to the brokenhearted and saves those who are crushed in spirit.
Psalm 34:17-18 (NIV)

God, since you rejected some of my requests my life has been redirected. At first, I was mad, hurt, and confused as to why you would allow disappointments to happen in my life. Now, I see it was for my good. I was heading down the path of death, and you placed me back in the lane of life. Nobody could have done it but you.

Today, I just want to thank you. Thank you for refusing to agree with some of the decisions I make. Thank you for answering my prayers in a better way than I prayed them. Thank you for not subjecting me to my sins. God, thank you for hearing more than what I pray for. You hear my hopes, fears, and intentions. Thank you for being the filter, removing things that I do not need.

In Jesus' name, I pray. Amen.

Success and Sacrifice

Then Jesus beholding him loved him, and said unto him,
one thing thou lackest: go thy way, sell whatsoever thou
hast, and give to the poor, and thou shalt have treasure in
heaven: and come, take up the cross, and follow me.
Mark 10:21 (KJV)

Dear God, I am going to have to sacrifice some things to be
more successful. A new level of success is going to require for
me to give myself away to you.

God, help me to stop spending time with certain people who
mean me no good. I pray that you remove the desire from me
to go places I use to go. Change me God and make me more
like you. Prepare me to make the necessary sacrifices needed
to go to a higher level.

Lord, I surrender to you. I give my bad habits and what
appears as good habits over to you for review. Take away
anything that hinders me from being in your will. I do not
want success without sacrifice. For I know that I grow when I
am stretched beyond my comfort zone.
God, stretch me today.

In Jesus' name, I pray. Amen.

Love God

And now, Israel, what doth the Lord thy God require of
thee, but to fear the Lord thy God, to walk in all his ways,
and to love him, and to serve the Lord thy God with all
thy heart and with all thy soul.
Deuteronomy 10:12 (KJV)

God, I love you because you were the first person to love me.
God, no one else can love as you do. You love me in spite of
all my faults. I love your unmerited favor, sufficient grace,
and matchless mercy. I love how you are a life changer. I love
your patience with me. Most importantly, I love you for who
you are. If you decide to stop doing things for me, I will still
love you. You have done enough just by sending your son to
die that I may have the right to live. I love you forever and
always through pain and gain.

Today, I pray that you teach me to love you in return. Show
me how I should live my life so that you are pleased with it. I
decree that the death of Jesus' is not in vain. I will live and
love in the way he purposed for me when he died.

In Jesus' name, I pray. Amen.

See the Goodness

I remain confident of this: I will see the goodness of the
Lord in the land of the living.
Psalm 27:13 (NIV)

I am alive today, so I know that your goodness is with me.
Today is the day that you have made; I will rejoice and be
glad! For today, I will not be overcome by evil, but with
good, I will overcome evil as it says in Romans 12:21.

God, as I pray to you, I feel your goodness all over me. You
are my keeper, my sustainer, and my guide. I believe that
your goodness and love will follow me today, tomorrow, and
every day after. I declare that I will experience all you have
for me while I am still alive. I believe your goodness has
reached me at this very moment.

I pray that you grant me every blessing here on earth before I
dwell in heaven with you.

In Jesus' name, I pray. Amen.

The Word

And they overcame him by the blood of the Lamb, and by the word of their testimony; and they loved not their lives unto the death.
Revelation 12:11 (KJV)

God, give me the courage to share my life experiences. I believe that you turned my experiences into testimonies that I may tell others about your goodness. Someone maybe depending on me to live fearlessly in my truth so they can explore living in theirs. God rebuke every thought that crosses my mind and tells me to conceal your goodness towards me.

God, I repent for allowing fear to control my tongue. God, I thank you for reinstalling boldness and courage to me. I decree and declare that I will not live in secrecy. My past is the past, but it built me to last. Free me from feeling conceited and vain. Show me how to share my experiences with others in a motivating way, so that they are inspired.

In Jesus' name, I pray. Amen.

Three Days Left

Cast thy burden upon the Lord, and he shall sustain thee:
he shall never suffer the righteous to be moved.
Psalm 55:22 (KJV)

God, this has been a year of growth. I may not yet see it or feel it, but I decree that growth has taken place in me. Today, I give you everything in me that tried to hold me back from being victorious.

I pray that you fill me with everything I need to go to a higher level in my faith. In the last three days of this year, I believe you are going to move in my life. I decree and declare freedom, protection, and favor. God, do not let me go into this next year without your guidance. Do not let me go into this new year with baggage from previous ones.

I give you my past pain that caused me to live in fear of the future. I give you my financial problems and the pressures to keep up. I give you every ounce of depression, low self-esteem, envy, greed, anger, and lust that may be housed in my body. Every scar, flashback, and the residue of sin I dump it at your feet. I give you my sorrows, regrets, negative thoughts, and tendencies. I throw pride, stubbornness, and jealousy at your feet. I give you every tear, every sleepless night, and lazy morning.

God, I am empty and ready to be filled with your Spirit. Fill me up with the things you desire for me. I declare that the end of this year is the beginning of a new year with freedom, protection, and favor.

In Jesus' name, I pray. Amen.

No Prayer, No Power | Amber R. Morson

Yet Will I Praise

Praise the Lord, my soul, and forget not all his benefits.
Psalm 103:2 (NIV)

This year has been a roller coaster ride. I was up then the next thing I knew I was being let down. However, I am happy because I am here today. The benefit of your grace has kept me. I see now that no storm last forever even when it feels like it will.

God, I choose to maximize the high moments of this year. I thank you that through thick and thin I had someone to stick it through with me. I praise you because things could have been much worse. I could still be in the storm, struggling, and frustrated, but you saw fit to rescue me.

Never again will I focus on what looks bad and disregard the good. In the coming year, I pray that you help me to focus on what I do have. God, you are good, and your goodness deserves my attention and praise. Thank you for working things out. Forgive me for complaining about things you already have under control.

In Jesus' name, I pray. Amen.

1 Am Happy

*A happy heart makes the face cheerful, but heartache
crushes the spirit.*
Proverbs 15:13 (NIV)

God, I find my happiness in you. You are my hope. You are
my peace. You are my joy and the source of my laughter. It is
no greater feeling than knowing that you love me. In the
midst of everything I go through one thought of you makes
me happy.

I am happy because I know your word is true. I pray that you
block me from getting in the way of my own happiness. Do
not let me go into a new year dwelling on the past and
pressures of life. The pressure is purposeful and it is going to
take me somewhere.

I decree and declare that I will practice being happy until
happiness becomes a habit. I declare that I will have
happiness for the remainder of every year to come.

In Jesus' name, I pray. Amen.

Get the Glory God

Thine, O Lord is the greatness, and the power, and the glory, and the victory, and the majesty: for all that is in the heaven and in the earth is thine; thine is the kingdom, O Lord, and thou art exalted as head above all.
1 Chronicles 29:13 (KJV)

God, you are Lord over all. You are great, victorious, and magnificent. You hold strength and power in the palm of your hands. In the same hands, you hold me. I have become so much stronger and wiser because you kept me. I am so unworthy of all the things you have done for me. I do not deserve your love or loyalty. I did nothing to deserve your mercy and grace.

God, I sincerely thank you for allowing me to see this day. Millions did not make it, but I did. I will not take the opportunity for an upcoming new year for granted. I will continue to press on until your glory is revealed in me.

In Jesus' name, I pray. Amen.

40042303R00205

Made in the USA
Lexington, KY
24 May 2019